W. H. Davenport Adams

Our Native Land - New Series

Windsor Castle and the Water-way Thither

W. H. Davenport Adams

Our Native Land - New Series
Windsor Castle and the Water-way Thither

ISBN/EAN: 9783744791687

Printed in Europe, USA, Canada, Australia, Japan

Cover: Foto ©ninafisch / pixelio.de

More available books at **www.hansebooks.com**

OUR NATIVE LAND.—NEW SERIES.

WINDSOR CASTLE

AND THE

WATER-WAY THITHER

BY

W. H. DAVENPORT ADAMS

AUTHOR OF "THE ARCTIC WORLD," "THE MEDITERRANEAN ILLUSTRATED," &c.

WITH SEVENTY-FOUR ILLUSTRATIONS BY R. T. PRITCHETT
AND TWELVE WATER-COLOUR SKETCHES AFTER F. JONES.

London:
MARCUS WARD & CO., 67 & 68, CHANDOS STREET
AND ROYAL ULSTER WORKS, BELFAST
1880

CONTENTS.

CHAP.		PAGE
I.	General Description of the Thames—Battersea—Fulham—Putney—Chiswick—Mortlake—Kew—Kew Gardens	1
II.	Brentford—Richmond Hill—Richmond Park—The Bridge and Town—Ham House	9
III.	Eel-pie Island—Twickenham—Twickenham Church—Pope's Villa—Orleans House—Strawberry Hill—Teddington—Kingston—Kingston Church—Thames Ditton—Esher—Wolsey's Tower—Claremont	17
IV.	Hampton Court Palace—History of the Palace—The Gardens—The Vinery—Bushey Park	25
V.	Molesey—Garrick Villa—Sunbury—Halliford—Walton—Mount Felix—Walton Church—Scold's Bridle—Walton Bridge—Oatlands Park	34
VI.	Weybridge—Weybridge Church—Shepperton—Chertsey—Cowley's House—Chertsey Church—Chertsey Abbey—Laleham—Ponton Hook—Staines—Egham—Cooper's Hill—Runnimede—Charter Island—Englefield Green	41
VII.	Horton—Old Windsor—Datchet—Old Windsor Lock—Windsor Town—Views of the Castle—The Great Park—The Lodges—The Home Park—Herne's Oak—Frogmore House—Prince Consort's Mausoleum	49
VIII.	History of Windsor Castle—Henry I. at Windsor—Erection of the Round Tower—Order of the Garter—Death of Queen Philippa—The Poet-King, James of Scotland—The King's Quhair—Imprisonment of Charles, Duke of Orleans—Henry of Windsor—Erection of St. George's Chapel—The Lord of Granthuse's Picture of Windsor—Burial of Edward IV.—Anne Boleyn—Burial of Henry VIII.—The Poet-Earl of Surrey	58
IX.	Virginia Water—Its Creation—The Grotto—Fishing Temple—Royal Visits to Virginia Water	73
X.	Windsor: its later History—Elizabeth at Windsor—Hentzner's Description of Windsor and the Queen—Funeral of Charles I.—Charles II.—James II.—Anne—Duke of Gloucester—His Death—Routine of Queen Anne's life—Miss Burney's Account of Queen Charlotte—Mrs. Delany's Sketches of Windsor—A Windsor Interior—Enlargements by George III.—George IV. at the Royal Lodge—The Account in Mr. Greville's "Diary"—Baron Bunsen's Account of Windsor in 1846—Ballad History of Windsor	75
XI.	Windsor Castle as it is—Lower Ward—St. George's Chapel—The Choir—Memorial Window—Queen's Closet—A Garter Festival—Bray Chapel—Rutland Chapel—Lincoln Chapel—Oxenbridge Chapel—Hastings Chapel—Aldworth Chapel—Beaufort Chapel—Urswick Chapel—Memorial Chapel—Dean's Cloisters—Middle Ward—View from the Round Tower—The "Maiden's Tower"—Upper Ward—Audience Chamber—The Vandyck Room—State Drawing-Room—State Ante-Room—Grand Staircase and Vestibule—Waterloo Chamber—Grand Ball-Room—St. George's Hall—Guard Chamber—The Armoury—Queen's Presence Chamber—The Rubens Room—King's Closet—Queen's Closet—Council Chamber—Throne-Room—State-Rooms—Plate-Room—Royal Library	97
XII.	Eton College—Its History—Description of the Building—"Montem" Day—Upton Church—Stoke Pogis Church—Gray's Elegy—Gray's Monument—Burnham Beeches	121

ILLUSTRATIONS.

	PAGE		PAGE
Putney Bridge and Church by Moonlight	2	Windsor at Sunrise (from the Brocas)	69
Windmill on Wimbledon Common	4	Windsor Lasher	71
Chiswick	5	The Bell-Tower—Saturday	75
Hammersmith Bridge	8	Iron Letters, North Walk	76
Old Houses at Brentford	9	Lead Work on Ramparts, Round Tower	76
Remains of Richmond Palace	12	Do. do. do.	76
White Lodge, Richmond Park	13	Stone Work on Ramparts, Round Tower	79
The Thames, from Ham House	16	Do. do. do.	79
Twickenham	17	Capital on Ramparts, Round Tower	79
Kingston Church and Bridge	20	Knocker at No. 10 Cloister	79
Esher Church	22	The Cloisters above the Steps	81
Wolsey's Tower	23	The Throne-Room, Windsor	83
Claremont	24	Horse-shoe Cloisters	88
Entrance to Hampton Court Palace	25	St. George's Chapel, West End	89
Ancient Sun-dial at Hampton Court	33	The Waterloo Chamber	92
Molesey Weir	34	Old Sculptured Arms	96
Sunbury Church	35	The Winchester Tower	98
Scold's Bridle	36	The Norman Gate	99
Walton Bridge	38	The Queen's Closet	101
Coway Stakes	39	Albert Memorial Chapel	106
Old Pump, Walton	40	The Dean's Cloisters	108
Weybridge, from Shepperton	41	View from Round Tower, Lower Rampart	109
Confluence of the Wey and Thames	42	The "Maiden's Tower"	111
Chertsey	43	Windsor, from the East Approach	115
Ponton Hook	45	Windsor, from Clewer	117
View from Cooper's Hill	46	Spanish Wine-Flagon	120
Shepperton	48	Burnham Beeches	121
Prince Consort's Tomb	49	Church Staircase, Eton	122
Victoria Bridge	50	Head Master's Room, Eton College	125
Datchet	51	Gray's Tomb	129
Black Pots	53	Boat-Houses, Eton	130
Windsor Castle, from the River	54	Lower School, Eton	136
Windsor Castle, from the Long Walk	55	The "Lupton" Badges, Eton College Chapel	137
End of the Long Walk	56	Upton Church	140
Mausoleum	57	Stoke Pogis Church	141
Old Windsor Lock	59	Church Porch, Stoke Pogis	142
Windsor Castle, from the Park	66	Gray's Monument	144

CHROMOGRAPHS.

	PAGE		PAGE
View from Richmond Hill	1	Ruins in Windsor Park	73
Richmond Bridge	8	Windsor Castle	80
Hampton Court Palace	25	St. George's Chapel	97
Long Walk, Windsor Park	32	Round Tower, Windsor	104
Lake at Virginia Water	49	Eton College	121
Cascade at Virginia Water	56	Quadrangle of Eton College	128

CHAPTER I.

FROM BATTERSEA TO KEW.

ALL scenery worthy of the name has a character of its own which distinguishes it from other scenery of the same kind, though it may not be superior—perhaps, from some points of view, not even equal—to it. Attempts at comparison, therefore, must generally prove futile or misleading. It is surely a mark of the most ignorant fanaticism to insist, as many will do, on the greater beauty and more stirring interest of the landscapes of the Rhine as compared with those of the Thames; or to see a profound charm in the mountain-bosomed lochs of the Clyde, and none in the pastoral reaches and gently-curving uplands of our chief English river. The truth is, the Thames has its special and peculiar features of attraction; and as much may be said of the Clyde or the Rhine. There are landscapes in the neighbourhood of Cookham, Goring, and Pangbourne which cannot be surpassed even in the lower valley of the Clyde. But then they are wholly unlike those which embellish the latter; they form a contrast, not a comparison; and to discuss them in relation to each other would be as unwise as to institute a comparison between Shakespeare and Milton. Let us have eyes for each, and thank Heaven for both. Or if, while we gaze on the purple hills through which the estuary of the Clyde rolls its shining waters, our souls are moved to declare that earth can show nothing more beautiful, let us affirm the same just as enthusiastically when we trace the silver windings of the Thames through gentle dales, crowned with luxuriant foliage. The lover of Nature professes a wise catholicity. He will be a Frenchman on the banks of the Loire; a German minnesinger in presence of the "chiefless castles, breathing stern farewells," which frown gloomily from the summit of the heights and headlands of the Rhine. A thing of beauty appeals to his imagination as strongly on the wide prairies of the Mississippi as on the profuse plains of the Ganges. He does not trouble himself to draw up a catalogue of the sights which move his fancy, arranging them in some arbitrary order of merit—the first place to

A

this, and the second place to that, and the third place to another; but he knows that all are good, and his heart goes forth to all with an equal affection.

Professing the same catholicity, we have no intention to depreciate other rivers in order to exalt the Thames, or to depreciate the Thames in order to aggrandise its supposed rivals. We love them all—Clyde, Tay, Tweed, Don, Severn, Tamar, Dart, and Avon. We say that each has a beauty peculiar, and, so to speak, indigenous to itself. But, in justice to the Thames, we would object to the charge of monotony that is sometimes levelled at it. To him who will go far enough afield, the variety of the Thames will be sufficiently notable. It has, as at Cliffe, its lofty bluffs of chalk, rising erect like a sea-washed promontory. It has its broad stretches of level marsh, dotted with fat cattle, like a picture by Cuyp or Hobbema. It has its strange, quaint hostelries, and obscure wharves and landing-places, over which broods an atmosphere of mystery, suggestive of tales of suffering and crime. It has its huge docks,

PUTNEY BRIDGE AND CHURCH BY MOONLIGHT.

crowded with tall masts, which speak of a commerce extending over every sea. It has its long lines of quays, and streets, and factories, and its wide-arched bridges, all indicating the wealth and business-activity of the great metropolis through which it rolls its tide. Its waters reflect the shifting shadows, by night and day, of stately palaces, of tall-spired churches, and gardens green with lawn and tree. It sweeps past the terraces of many an ancient wall and mansion, rich in associations with the men that made England great, and the events that have built up her structure of freedom and independence. It flows through fertile meadows, which wave with luxuriant grass, and curves round the base of wooded knolls, and murmurs sleepily in the deep shadows of interwoven boughs. Its silver-winding way takes it within sight of tranquil villages which seem still absorbed in the old world order; "by hedgerow elms, on hillocks green;" in the shade of old church towers and ruined minsters; and wherever it goes it seems to bear with it the history of England, and its waters sing a continuous song of England's greatness.

We begin our present exploration of the Thames at Battersea. After passing the bridge, we see on our left hand a succession of factories and small, dull-looking houses, belonging to the town of Wandsworth, which has sprung up here at the confluence of the Wandle and the Thames. Its river-ward aspect is sufficiently uninviting; but in the opposite direction, towards Wandsworth Common, it assumes a more picturesque character, and can boast of numerous "villas" and "mansions," each in its compact belt of garden-ground. Its outlying hamlet of Garrett was formerly famous for a mock municipal election, the rude humours of which have been severely satirised by Foote in his farce, "The Mayor of Garrett."

On the Middlesex bank of the Thames we pass the site of "Cremorne," a once notorious place of public entertainment, and soon come in sight of the groves of pleasant Fulham, anciently Fullanhamme, or Fullenholme, "the place of birds." To this day, the name remains appropriate, as anyone can testify who has moved in the shade of the Fulham trees on a sunny April morning; and we decline to believe that it ought to be derived from *fule*, "foul and muddy," as Bosworth asserts. The quaint "palace" of the Bishop of London attracts us by the amenity of its situation. Close by is Fulham Church, in the sequestered graveyard of which sleeps the dust of many a right reverend and revered prelate. In a small house, which was removed to make way for the Water Company's hideous aqueduct, just above Putney Bridge, lived the wittiest of diners-out, and the most spontaneous of English improvisatores, Theodore Hook, a man who made but little profitable use, for himself or his fellows, of his large intellectual gifts. He lies buried in the churchyard, which also contains the dust of the Latinist, Vincent Bourne. Still higher up is Craven Cottage, the residence, for some years, of the late Lord Lytton, who, in striking contrast to Hook, cultivated his talents with the most unsparing assiduity, and so successfully that, as novelist, dramatist, essayist, and orator, he won a well-deserved reputation.

A narrow, inconvenient, and exceedingly ugly bridge of timber connects Fulham with Putney, a thriving metropolitan suburb, which still contrives to retain something of its whilom rural air. Pass through the village, ascend the hill, and enter upon the Common; you will be surprised at the pleasantness which pervades the scene. There are fine trees all around it; here and there clumps of gorse in the spring-time blossom into gold; the fresh air rings with the songs of birds. Handsome houses and elegant villas may be seen in every direction, and as all are surrounded with gardens and shrubberies, they by no means impair the general effect of the picture. A really delightful lane leads to Roehampton, and thence to the river-banks; and the walk across the common to Wimbledon can hardly fail to cheer and delight the pedestrian. As he wanders from point to point, he may recall some of the associations with which the place abounds. He may bethink himself of the duels which took place here (in May, 1798) between William Pitt and William Tierney, and (in September, 1809) between Lord Castlereagh and George Canning—the latter being shot in the thigh—and rejoice that the laws of honour no longer recognise a custom so absurd. Or he may direct his mind's eye to the interior of Putney Church, where, in 1647, Cromwell and his officers, after listening to a discourse of some favourite preacher, engaged in council. Or he may recollect that the wit, satirist, and dramatist, Douglas Jerrold, lived, from 1845 to 1854, at West Lodge on Putney Heath; and that at Bowling Green House died William Pitt, of a broken heart and a broken constitution, on the 23rd of January, 1806. Nicholas West, the baker's boy who rose to be Bishop of Ely, was a native of Putney. So was Thomas Cromwell, Earl of Essex, whom Aubrey cites as "a remarkable instance of the inconstancy of fortune." The son of "a blacksmith of this place," he was "raised from the anvil and forge to the most beneficial places, and highest honours in the nation." So, too, Putney gave birth to the historian of "The Decline and Fall of Rome." His house was situated between the roads which lead to Wandsworth and Wimbledon. The farm and pleasure-grounds which adjoined the house were very spacious, containing nearly eighty acres, and commanding a fine prospect in all directions. Our illustration will be familiar to the thousands who throng

WINDMILL ON WIMBLEDON COMMON.

to see or take part in the great Volunteer Encampment which yearly forms around the old windmill on Wimbledon Common.

Returning to the river, we pass the "Star and Garter," the head-quarters of Thames amateur oarsmen, the starting-point (above the aqueduct) of the Oxford and Cambridge boat-race, and the club-house of the London Rowing Club, and quickly arrive at Hammersmith Suspension Bridge, constructed in 1828 from the designs of W. Tierney Clarke. Hammersmith Church, an edifice of considerable pretension, was built by Sir Nicholas Crispe, a London merchant, in the reign of Charles I. He remained faithful to his king during the long struggle between the Crown and the Parliament, and found his reward in the epitaph engraved upon his monument:—
"Within this urn is entombed the heart of Sir Nicholas Crispe, Knt. and Baronet, a loyal sharer in the sufferings of his late and present Majesty. He first settled the trade of gold from Guinea, and there built the castle of Connantine. Died there 26th July, 1665, aged 67 years."

Also, on the Middlesex side of the river, and just above Hammersmith, lies the pretty village of Chiswick, half hidden, like a bird's nest, among embowering foliage. It is famous in the world of society for the recherché entertainments given by successive Dukes of Devonshire—with whom courtesy and hospitality are a tradition of the race—at Chiswick House, which, with its delightful gardens, is one of the most charming "retreats" in the vicinity of London. The house was designed and built by Richard, Earl of Burlington, and assumes the character of a stately Italian villa.* The great attraction of the place, however, lies in the beautiful grounds, which are richly diversified with grove, lawn, and pasture, and remind the spectator of "a picture by Watteau," or of that romantic garden in Boccaccio's "Decameron," where the gay Florentine ladies sang and made merry. Chiswick, nevertheless, in spite of the gaiety and light laughter that have prevailed beneath its leafy canopies, has its melancholy associations. Here died Charles James Fox, on the 13th of September, 1806; and in the same room died George Canning, on the 8th of August, 1827.

CHISWICK.

We must not leave Chiswick without a peep into its picturesque graveyard, which contains the dust of not a few remarkable men and women—as, for instance, that of the handsome, imperious, and voluptuous Duchess of Cleveland, Charles II.'s mistress, a woman of many vices, but not wholly insensible to generous impulses; of Mary, the third, and Frances, the youngest daughter of Oliver Cromwell; of the Italian exile, poet, and commentator on Dante, Ugo Foscolo; that of the painter, Loutherbourg; the actor, Holland; and the diplomatist, Lord Macartney, England's first ambassador to the Court of Pekin. Nor must we forget the grave of William Hogarth, the painter-moralist, who used his brush to paint and satirise the follies and weaknesses of humanity, and made his canvas reflect, as in a mirror, the vices of his time.

---

* When first built, Lord Hervey said of it, "it was too small to inhabit, and too large to hang to one's watch-chain." One of the Dukes of Devonshire enlarged it by the addition of two wings.

ABOUT BARN-ELMS.

It is especially noticeable in this conservative England of ours, that the Old and the New are constantly found in the closest contiguity; the Present linking itself on to the Past, as if anxious to seek and secure its support. Next door to a shining modern mansion, with plate-glass windows and all the latest improvements, may be seen a relic of the old times, a quaint, timber-built house, with latticed casements, and a cloud of ivy creeping up its sides and over its roof. On the outskirts of a great city, within hearing of the restless wheels of mill or factory, will crumble away the grey walls and lichened buttresses of castle or abbey. Something of this interesting combination of the ancient and the modern, which bears such vivid testimony to the continuity of English history, meets us at Barnes. Yonder modernised Elizabethan mansion is the famous Barn-Elms, where, in 1589, Queen Elizabeth visited Sir Francis Walsingham, and was received with all the pomp and pageantry she so much affected; processions by land and water, nymphs and pages, heralds with courtly verses, and strains of lively music. It was afterwards the residence of Sir Henry Wyat, and, at a later period, of the poet Cowley. In a neighbouring field or meadow was fought, on the 17th of January, 1667-68, an infamous duel between Villiers, Duke of Buckingham, and the Earl of Shrewsbury, the cause being the latter's wanton Countess, who, it is said, held her lover's horse while he dealt the death-blow to her injured husband. Fielding, the novelist, "Monk" Lewis, and Handel, resided for a while at Barnes. At Barnes Terrace, E. W. Cooke, R.A., painted some of his most popular pictures. Portions of the church are reputed to be as old as the time of Richard Cœur-de-Lion.

We now come in sight of the low level of Mortlake, Aubrey's "Mortlac," the name of which is traced, by some ingenious etymologists, to the Latin *Mortuus lacus*, "the dead lake." The Archbishops of Canterbury had formerly a manorial mansion or palace here, which witnessed the Whitsuntide festival of the saintly Anselm in 1099, and the deaths of Archbishop Peckham in 1292, and Walter Reynolds in 1327. A tapestry manufactory was established at Mortlake in 1619 by the ingenious Sir Francis Crane. Charles I., as became so intelligent a patron of the Fine Arts, patronised it warmly, and commissioned the proprietor to copy for him in tapestry five of Raffaelle's cartoons. Both Rubens and Vandyck were employed by Crane as designers. The tapestry works occupied the site of the laboratory of the once celebrated wizard, Dr. Dee, who, on more than one occasion, was visited by Queen Elizabeth. He exhibited to her curious Majesty the "rock-crystal," or "show-stone," by means of which he professed to communicate with his "familiars." *

Mortlake Church, which is visible from the river, boasts a noble tower. Here lie buried Lord Sidmouth, Canning's "Doctor Addington," at one time Prime Minister

---

* A polished sphere of smoke-coloured rock-crystal, about the size of a billiard-ball, may be seen in the British and Mediæval Room at the British Museum. It is labelled—"Dr. Dee's Show-stone. See Sir Walter Scott's *Demonology and Witchcraft*."

of England; Sir Philip Francis, whom some authorities regard as the author of the "Letters of Junius," though the arguments they adduce have been shown by Mr. Hayward to be deficient in substance; Partridge, the almanack-maker; and the Sir John Barnard, Lord Mayor of London, whose philanthropy has been eulogised by Pope.

With a deep wide curve the river next brings us, on the Surrey bank, to Kew, where a green little eyot, or islet, in mid-stream, forms a sufficiently pleasant object Kew Bridge is a plain structure of seven arches. The Railway Station is situated near the Middlesex end.

The village of Kew, containing some interesting old houses, surrounds the Green, an open breadth of turf, kept always in excellent order. This Green has justly been described as "one of the most quaint and peculiar bits of scenery within ten miles of the metropolis. The Church may be taken as the principal feature—a clean, bright, stately English church, neither new nor old. The Green is irregularly flanked by houses of all heights and qualities; some trellised, some bare and stately, others hid away in the bright foliage which climbs their walls; some standing boldly forward others hiding modestly behind trees." It is reported that the organ in Kew Church belonged to Handel, and was a favourite instrument of George III.'s, in his dark days of mental despondency. Gainsborough, one of the greatest of English artists, lies buried in Kew Churchyard.

Sir Peter Lely, whose brush was so often employed to transfer to glowing canvas the charms of the frail beauties of Charles II.'s court, had a house upon the Green.

Kew Palace, a favourite residence of George III., is still standing. It is an old Tudor building of red brick, dating from the reign of Elizabeth; and appears to have undergone little change since it was occupied by "the farmer King." At Kew House, pulled down in 1802, he had previously resided for about three months every year, he and his family throwing off all affectation of royal state, and living like "the simplest country gentlefolks."

After the attack upon George III.'s life by Margaret Nicholson, the lunatic, in August, 1786, the good people of Kew exhibited an "exceedingly pretty scene" of loyal sympathy. Says our diarist:—"We came, as usual on every alternate Tuesday, to Kew. The Queen's Lodge is at the end of a long meadow, surrounded with houses, which is called Kew Green; and this was quite filled with all the inhabitants of the place—the lame, old, blind, sick, and infants—who all assembled, dressed in their Sunday garb, to line the sides of the roads through which their Majesties passed, attended by a band of musicians, arranged in the front, who began 'God save the King' the moment they came upon the Green, and finished it with loud huzzas. This was a compliment at the expense of the better inhabitants, who paid the musicians themselves, and mixed in with the group, which, indeed, left not a soul, I am told, in any house in the place."

The Botanic Gardens at Kew are a favourite resort with London holiday-makers, no less than with horticultural amateurs or botanical students. They are open daily from noon till sunset, except on Sundays, when the hours are from two till seven. We have no space to describe them fully or fitly; and, indeed, they belong to that class of exhibitions of which no verbal descriptions can give a satisfactory idea. Within their comparatively limited area are gathered the botanical treasures of the earth; plants of all countries and of all climates, the denizens of Eastern jungles, of Southern islands, of Alpine heights. The great Palm-House, designed by Decimus Burton, and erected in 1845-8, a shining hall of crystal 362 feet long and 100 feet wide, with transepts of proportionate dimensions, is crowded with a tropical luxuriance of foliage, remarkable alike for variety of form and diversity of colour. Here you may see the giant banyan, the Madagascar tanghin or poison-tree, the New Zealand screw-pine, the esculent mango, the Egyptian papyrus, the cassava and the sugar-cane, the cocoa-tree—renowned for grace and utility—the date palm, wax palm, ivory palm, sago palm, and broad-leaved fern palm; the gum dragon, or dragon's blood tree, the areca, cinnamon, cotton, silk, mahogany. In a conservatory near the entrance is stored a fine collection of Australian trees and plants. The Victoria House enshrines a good specimen of the stately Victoria Regia. The hardier conifers are collected in the Pinetum; and suitable houses are devoted to orchids, heaths, Amherstias, tropical ferns, and New Zealand productions. There are also Rhododendron, Camellia, and Aroidaceous houses, and to this extensive collection additions are constantly being made.

HAMMERSMITH BRIDGE.

RICHMOND BRIDGE

CHAPTER II.

BRENTFORD—RICHMOND—HAM HOUSE.

OLD HOUSES AT BRENTFORD.

BEYOND Kew Bridge, on the Middlesex bank of the river, stretches the squalid-looking town of Brentford,* with its gas-works, factories, and distilleries, and its congeries of dirty streets and narrow alleys. "The Three Pigeons" seen here was once a notable hostelry; its landlord, John Lowen, belonged to Shakespeare's company of players, and enacted Sir John Falstaff. In the neighbourhood lie extensive market-gardens, which furnish occupation to a large number of persons. We pass next to Isleworth, the ancient ivy-covered tower of its parish church forming a picturesque landmark. The body of the building is of red brick, and dates from 1705, but contains some monumental brasses transferred from the more ancient edifice. One of these represents the figure of "Margaret Dely, a syster professed in Syon," who died in 1561, and must, therefore, have been one of the very last of English nuns. Sion House, the seat of the Duke of Northumberland, stands close to the church, on the site of the ancient convent of Bridgetine nuns. Here Queen Catherine Howard was imprisoned, prior to her trial for unfaithfulness to her capricious sovereign and husband; and here Lady Jane Grey reluctantly accepted the crown which proved so fatal a burden. The present mansion was built in the early years of James I. It forms a plain, unpretending quadrangular pile of stone.

The gardens of Kew line the Surrey bank of the river for about two miles, and where they end Richmond begins. This is one of the fairest parts of the Thames

---

* "Brentford's tedious town,
For dirty streets and white-legged chickens known."—GAY.

A FAIR LANDSCAPE.

scenery; wood and water, swelling hill, stately terrace, and masses of garden-bloom combining to form a vivid and luxurious picture. Whether our point of view be the summit of Richmond Hill, or the Bridge, or the terrace walks along the river-bank, we cannot but admire the singular richness of the landscapes that greet us on every hand. That they have nothing of the sublime, picturesque, or majestic about them, may be admitted; but in tranquil loveliness, in the beauty that wins by its softness and tenderness of character, they are unsurpassed.

Let us first betake ourselves to the crest of Richmond Hill. The extensive and varied view which it commands has inspired Turner with one of his finest landscapes, and Thomson with one of the most glowing passages of his "Seasons." The poet exclaims—

> "Here let us sweep
> The boundless landscape : and the raptured eye,
> Exulting, swift to huge Augusta send,
> Now to the sister hills* that skirt her plain ;
> To lofty Harrow now, and now to where
> Majestic Windsor lifts his princely brow.
> In lovely contrast to this glorious view,
> Calmly magnificent, then will we turn
> To where the silver Thames first rural grows.
> There let the feasted eye unwearied stray ;
> Luxurious there, rove through the pendent woods
> That nodding hang o'er Harrington's retreat : †
> And, stooping thence to Ham's embow'ring walks,
> Slow let us trace the matchless vale of Thames ;
> Far winding up to where the Muses haunt
> In Twick'nam's bowers, to royal Hampton's pile,
> To Clermont's terraced height, and Esher's groves."

A briefer but scarcely less enthusiastic description occurs in Scott's "Heart of Mid-Lothian." The novelist represents the Duke of Argyle and Jeanie Deans as on their way to Richmond Palace. After passing through a pleasant village, he says, the equipage stopped on a commanding eminence, where the beauty of English landscape was displayed in its utmost luxuriance. The Duke alighted, and Jeanie followed his example. Then, for a moment, they paused on the brow of a hill to gaze on the unrivalled landscape which it presented. "A huge sea of verdure, with crossing and intersecting promontories of massive and tufted groves, was tenanted by numberless flocks and herds, which seemed to wander unrestrained and unbounded through the rich pastures. The Thames, here turreted with villas and there garlanded with forests, moved on slowly and placidly, like the mighty monarch of the scene, to whom all its other beauties were but accessories, and bore on its bosom an hundred barks and skiffs whose white sails and gaily fluttering pennons gave life to the whole."

The Hill rises from the river-bank with a slope gradual and easy from the old

---
* Highgate and Hampstead.   † Petersham House, long ago pulled down.

town, but steep from the river to the terrace stretched along the summit. Behind the terrace is a row of houses and hotels, from the windows of which the spectator looks out upon the dense masses of foliage that cover the whole valley underneath, and almost hide the winding course of the flashing Thames. Occasional breaks in this rich deep-green curtain reveal the summer palaces that line the foot of the hill, and afford glimpses of gay shallops that dart past from lawn-bordered coves and leafy creeks, and go on their way to the sound of music or the ripple of merry voices. The radiance of gardens is not wanting to complete the fairy-like picture, the effect of which is enhanced when the spectator ascends to a point commanding a fuller view of the sweep of the shining river. When he has satisfied himself with the bright scenes that lie close at hand, he may extend his survey to the distant horizon. The stately towers of royal Windsor are visible across Richmond Park; further off, the deep shadows of the beech-woods cover the rounded slopes of the Chilterns; nearer, the green hills of Surrey stretch down to the historic plain of Runnymede and the fair town of Chertsey. Eastward, the eye rests on many of the eminences which, embracing the arms and reaches of the Lower Thames, "fling their shadows on the sails of a hundred nations." Regarding this glorious combination of the most poetical elements of pastoral scenery, we may well pronounce it unequalled, or, at least, unsurpassed of its kind. There are three occasions on which it is seen to special advantage, so that it seems almost to pass out of this "terrestrial sphere" into an enchanted region of romance; namely, on a bright, clear morning in May, when the hawthorn is in bloom, and the air loaded with fragrance, and the birds attune "their sweetest notes." Again, by moonlight, when the scene is so softened and subdued by the silver lustre, that one cannot look upon it without a thrill of emotion; and yet again, on an autumn evening when the fires of the setting sun light up the many-coloured groves with a strange, indescribable glory.

We pass from Richmond Hill, not unmindful of the sonnet which Wordsworth has dedicated to it:—

"Fame tells of groves—from England far away—
Groves that inspire the nightingale to trill
And modulate, with subtle reach of skill
Elsewhere unmatch'd, her ever-varying lay;
Such bold report I venture to gainsay;
For I have heard the quire of Richmond Hill
Chanting, with indefatigable bill,
Strains that recalled to mind a distant day
When, haply, under shade of that same wood,
And scarcely conscious of the dashing oars
Plied steadily between those willowy shores,
The sweet-souled Poet of the Seasons stood—
Listening, and listening long, in rapturous mood,
Ye heavenly birds! to your progenitors."

English literature is so rich in great names, and English history so abounds in memorable events, that there is scarce a mile of ground in "Our Native Land" without its picturesque or stirring associations. Wherever we go, we come in contact with memorials of celebrated men, or traditions of remarkable incidents. Richmond, which to the ordinary visitor seems a place of fashionable resort, glittering with newness, and alive with gaiety, is affluent in such recollections. Just consider what and how much of historic interest clings to yonder old gateway of stone, with the arms of England carved above it, which ornaments the famous Green. It is almost the sole remains of Sheen or Richmond Palace, which Edward III. is said to have founded. Beneath its stately roof, deserted by his courtiers and robbed by his mistress, the old king died

REMAINS OF RICHMOND PALACE.

in 1377. There too, fourteen years later, expired the good queen, Anne of Bohemia, to the great grief of her distracted husband, Richard II., who, besides pouring out his curses upon the place where she died, "did also for anger throw down the buildings unto which the former kings, being wearied of the citie, used customarily to resort, as to a place of pleasure, and serving highly for recreation." Henry IV. rebuilt the palace on a splendid scale; and there, in May, 1492, Henry VII. "held a great and valiant jousting, the which endured by the space of a moneth, sometime within the sayde place, and sometime without, upon the greene without the gate of the said manor." Fire destroyed a considerable portion of the royal palace, but its immediate restoration was ordered, and it then received the name of "Richmond" instead of that of "Sheen," which it had previously borne. Here Henry VII. closed his chequered career in 1509; and here Henry VIII. received the great Emperor Charles V. It was a frequent residence with Queen Mary, and the scene of the death of Elizabeth. Charles I. seems to have been partial to it; but after the coming of William III. it fell into decay, and its site is now occupied by buildings of less distinction.

Richmond Park was first enclosed by Charles I. It is about nine miles in circumference, comprises 2250 acres, and extends into six parishes. Its surface is agreeably diversified; and the artist will find many charming "bits" for his pencil—clumps of aged and wide-spreading trees, and glistening lawns that slide down to broad pools of gleaming waters. The herds of deer add to the picturesque character of a landscape, which, beautiful and still and sylvan as it is, lies only ten miles from the metropolis of the world! If he would become properly acquainted with its various features, we recommend the visitor to enter the Park at Richmond Hill gate, turn to the right, keep along the road for a quarter of a mile, and then strike boldly across the turf and through the bracken, over the open park. He will presently find himself standing by the banks of a lake as perfectly wild as any in the backwoods of Canada. Heron fly over his head, and wild duck rise at the sound of his feet, with whirr of wings, to range themselves in their appointed order of flight in single file. If he sits motionless on the outstretched root of a tree, he will presently mark the rabbits coming timidly out of their holes, while the deer, not so tame as those in Greenwich Park, will gradually creep nearer. He might fancy himself a hundred miles from any human habitation. Yet large houses and smart mansions are situated within the precincts of the Park. On a well-wooded eminence stands the White Lodge, belonging to the Prince of Wales, but now occupied by the Duke and Duchess of Teck. It was formerly tenanted by Lord Sidmouth; and it still contains the small table upon which, in the course of an after-dinner conversation, Lord Nelson traced with his fingers his contemplated plan of attack when he next fell in with a French fleet—the plan which he carried out so successfully at Trafalgar. Pembroke Lodge was for many years the residence of that veteran statesman, the late Earl Russell. A grassy knoll within the grounds is called "King Harry's Mount," from an absurd tradition that Henry VIII. there waited to catch sight of the signal from Tower Hill announcing the death of Anne Boleyn. Professor Owen, one of the fathers of the science of comparative anatomy, lives at East Sheen Lodge.

WHITE LODGE, RICHMOND PARK.

Pursuing our researches, we come to the parish church, a spacious modernised structure, with a stately square tower of stone and flint. It contains numerous memorials of the dead; among others, tablets to Mrs. Yates, the tragic actress, and her husband, Richard Yates, the comedian, and to Gilbert Wakefield, the scholar. But we turn with eager eyes to the brass plate, simple as it is, which bears the name of James Thomson, the poet of "The Seasons," who died at Richmond, on the 22nd of August, 1748. It recalls to us the beautiful lines which the poet Collins dedicated to the memory of his friend and brother-minstrel:—

"In yonder grave a Druid lies,
  Where slowly winds the stealing wave;
The year's best sweets shall duteous rise,
  To deck its poet's sylvan grave.

"Remembrance oft shall haunt the shore,
  When Thames in summer-wreaths is drest;
And oft suspend the dashing oar,
  To bid his gentle spirit rest."

Outside the church, on its west front, is a marble tablet to Edmund Kean, who died at his house adjoining the Richmond Theatre, May 15, 1833.

Thomson lived in a cottage in Kewfoot Lane, with the rippling river in front, and a leafy garden behind. This cottage was afterwards embodied in a house built by a Mr. Ross, which in 1805 was bought by the Earl of Shaftesbury, and is now, much modified and enlarged, the Richmond Infirmary. Thomson's "Alcove," or summer-house, is still, we believe, in existence.

Along the river-walk we proceed to Richmond Bridge; a well-looking structure of ten arches, five of stone across the stream, and five of brick to provide for the escape of the swollen waters during the floods. It was erected in 1774-7. The river at this point is about 500 feet wide. In the sunny days of summer its surface is literally flecked with boats of all shapes and sizes, some bright with gilding and colours, some with sunny wings tossing like fairy shallops; while swift steam-launches dart merrily hither and thither, or a racing eight, propelled by nervous arms, shoots arrow-like through the crowd.

As for the town of Richmond, at one time celebrated for its composition of the savoury cakes called "Maids of Honour," it is so irregularly built as to baffle description. It contains numerous churches and chapels, first-class hotels and excellent inns, and is well supplied with good shops. The suburbs are embellished with mansions and villas of a "superior character," mostly situated in bright gardens of their own, and commanding a more or less extensive view of the scenery to which Richmond now owes its popularity.

We have no space to dwell on their details. The houses of the Duke of Buccleuch and the Marquis of Lansdowne are the most conspicuous; but among the more interesting are Downe House, where Sheridan lived; Heron Court, the residence of the late Lord Dalling; and Devonshire Cottage, associated with the memories of Lady Diana Beauclerk and the celebrated Georgiana, Duchess of Devonshire.

Just beyond the boundary of Richmond Park lies the straggling but picturesque hamlet of Petersham. Its church contains a memorial to one of England's sea-kings, Captain George Vancouver, "whose valuable and enterprising Voyage of Discovery to the North Pacific Ocean, and round the world, during twenty-five years of laborious survey, added greatly to the geographical knowledge of his countrymen." Here lie interred the remains of the two sisters, Mary and Agnes Berry, the friends of Horace Walpole, and the subjects of one of Lord Houghton's charming "Monographs." The inscription on their gravestone was written by the late Earl of Carlisle. The manor, as its name indicates, formerly belonged to the abbey of St. Peter's, Chertsey; was afterwards in the possession of Anne of Cleves; and, about 1637, was given to William Murray, Earl of Dysart. This nobleman's eldest daughter is one of the historic women of England. She married a Sir Lionel Tollemache: but being as ambitious as she was able, obtained from Charles II. the titles of Baroness Huntingtower and Countess of Dysart, with reversion to her heirs. Her character did not escape the tongue of scandal, and the gossips of the day connected her name with that of the great

Protector. "He was certainly fond of her," says Bishop Burnet, "and she took good care to entertain him in it." The Bishop adds, that she was endowed with a wonderful quickness of apprehension, and an amazing vivacity in conversation. She had studied not only history and divinity, but philosophy and mathematics. Her personal charms were considerable, and no doubt helped to secure her the political ascendency she loved. Over her second husband, the Duke of Lauderdale, who makes so sorry a figure in Scottish history, she exercised an undisputed power, and he ventured to do little without her advice or concurrence.

The residence of this imperious, unprincipled, and strong-minded woman was Ham House, the seat of the present Earl of Dysart, which now presents to us, as we pass up the river, the aspect of an ordinary Tudor mansion. It is built of red brick, and consists of a main body, ornamented by a range of oval niches, filled with stone-coloured busts of Roman and English worthies, and of two short wings, which project towards the river. In front of it stretches a broad and beautiful lawn, which encloses a huge allegorical carving of Father Thames, supported on a pedestal of rock. The great charm of the scene, however, lies in the long avenues of noble trees which cast their deep shadows far over the sloping sward, and extend for some distance along the river-side. It is said that the elm avenue suggested to Thomas Hood his striking poem of "The Elm Tree."

Ham House was built by Sir Thomas Vavasour, in 1610, for the use of Prince Henry, eldest son of James I., whose fatal illness is ascribed by tradition to his too frequent bathing in the Thames. Sir Thomas bequeathed his mansion to the Earl of Holderness, who sold it to the first Earl of Dysart, and then it passed on to the Earl's daughter, the masterful lady of whom we have already spoken. She expended large sums of money in decorating and furnishing it; hanging the walls with costly tapestry, and employing Verrio to embellish the ceilings with his liberal colours. Traces of the Countess's splendid taste are to be found in every apartment. The inlaid floors exhibit her cipher; and in an antechamber are preserved her walking-cane and desk. Her portrait, and the Duke's, by Sir Peter Lely, are shown in the Hall Gallery; and there are good specimens of Vandyck, Janssen, Sir Godfrey Kneller, and Sir Joshua Reynolds. Among the reliques which will attract the more thoughtful visitor are a lock of the hair of Queen Elizabeth's Earl of Essex, a prayer-book which belonged to Charles II., and another which belonged to Lady Rachel Russell.

Scotchmen will love to recollect that at Ham House, on the 10th of October, 1678, was born one of the most eminent of the race of Campbell, John, the great Duke of Argyle and Greenwich, alike distinguished as soldier and statesman. Pope commemorates him as

"Argyle, the State's whole thunder born to wield,
And shake alike the Senate and the Field."

We are told by a recent writer that so unchanged in its character is Ham House as to make but small demand upon the imagination to people it with the gay courtiers and light dames of the reign of the "Merry Monarch." Every object it contains is in harmony with the period: of modern furniture there is nothing; "but all the tables, chairs, footstools, fire-dogs—from things of curious and rare value down to the minutest matters of daily use—are of an age gone by." This advantage is mainly attributed to the fact that since the Restoration the venerable dwelling has had but few occupants— two of them, the Duchess of Lauderdale and the late Countess of Dysart, having died there when their years numbered upwards of fourscore. According to Hume, James II. was "ordered to retire to this house" on the arrival of the Prince of Orange in London, but he alleged (to quote Macaulay) "that he did not like Ham," that "it was a pleasant place in the summer, but cold and comfortless at Christmas," and he added that he should prefer Rochester. Subsequently, the manor-house at Ham ceased to possess any historic interest. Fortunately "there has been no wish on the part of its noble owners to effect 'restorations' of any kind; it has been consequently suffered to retain its solemn aspect and somewhat gloomy character; and remains a striking and impressive monument of the period of its erection."

The Duke of Lauderdale was the "L" of the famous "Cabal," a junta of five, who at one time exercised so disastrous an influence in the councils of Charles II. The other members were Clifford, Arlington, Buckingham, and Ashley. "By a mere coincidence," says Green, "the initials of these names formed the word 'Cabal,' which has ever since retained the sinister meaning their unpopularity gave to it." At Ham House is shown the Cabal Chamber, where the five councillors were accustomed to assemble in secret conclave. The walls are hung with tapestry from designs by Watteau. The readers of Dickens will remember that he places the scene of the fatal duel between Lord Frederick Verisopht and Sir Mulberry Hawk—the dupe and the duper—in the lonely fields behind Ham House.

THE THAMES FROM HAM HOUSE.

CHAPTER III.

TWICKENHAM TO KINGSTON AND ESHER.

TWICKENHAM.

WE must now carry the reader to the Middlesex side of our famous river, opposite which lies a large green ait, enclosed with shrubbery, and, under the name of Eel-pie Island, perennially popular with picnic parties, anxious to enjoy the staple fare provided at the Eel-pie Tavern. A narrow arm of the Thames separates it from the populous and well-built village of Twickenham, which was originally regarded as a hamlet of Isleworth, and held by the Brethren of the Holy Trinity, at Hounslow, and the Monks of Christ Church, Canterbury, until the dissolution of the Religious Houses. Afterwards it belonged to Henrietta Maria, the idolised wife of Charles I., and Catherine of Braganza, the neglected wife of Charles II. The names of the Earl of Rochester, the wit and poet, and Lord Bolingbroke, the statesman, are also connected with its ownership. Through its association with the poet Pope, it has realised the prediction of Horace Walpole, and become "as celebrated as Bath or Tivoli." The list of its worthies is, indeed, neither brief nor undistinguished; for it comprehends Lord Clarendon, the statesman; Horace Walpole; Hudson, Scott, and Sir Godfrey Kneller, the artists; Mrs. Clive and

Mrs. Pritchard, the actresses; with others of less repute. Some are enumerated by Walpole himself in his charming effusion, "The Parish Register of Twickenham":—

"Where silver Thames round Twit'nam meads
His winding current sweetly leads;
Twit'nam, the Muses' fav'rite seat,
Twit'nam, the Graces' loved retreat;
There polish'd Essex[a] wont to sport,
The pride and victim of a court;
There Bacon tun'd the grateful lyre,
To soothe Eliza's haughty ire. . . .
Twit'nam, where Hyde,[b] majestic sage,
Retir'd from folly's frantic stage;

Twit'nam, where frolic Wharton[c] revell'd;
Where Montague,[d] with locks dishevell'd,
(Conflict of dirt and warmth divine),
Invoked and scandalis'd the Nine;
Where Pope in moral music spoke
To th' anguish'd soul of Bolingbroke;
Where Fielding[e] met his Muse. . .
Where Suffolk[f] sought the peaceful scene,
Resigning Richmond to the Queen;
Where Fanny,[g] ever-blooming fair,
Ejaculates the graceful prayer."

Twickenham Church contains the memorials of Pope and his family. The poet's, of dark grey marble, pyramidal in form, and including a medallion and laurel wreath, was erected by Bishop Warburton. The inscription runs as follows:—

"**Porta Loquitur,**
"FOR ONE WHO WOULD NOT BE BURIED IN WESTMINSTER ABBEY.

"Heroes and kings, your distance keep,
In peace let our poor poet sleep;
Who never flattered folks like you;
Let Horace blush, and Virgil too."

Sir Godfrey Kneller is buried here, but without a memorial. Pope's monument to his parents is on the east wall, over the gallery. In the south gallery observe that to John, Lord Berkeley, of Stratton, died 1678, the hero of the conflict of Stratton Field. The epitaph upon Nathaniel Pigott, died 1737, was written by Pope. There are memorials to Admiral Sir Chaloner Ogle, died 1750; Richard Owen Cambridge, author of "The Scribleriad," died 1802; and (on the outer wall) to Kitty Clive, the actress, died 1758, erected by Miss Pope, a scarcely less illustrious ornament of the British stage. Admiral Byron, died 1786, whose well-known "Narrative of the Loss of the Wager" suggested to his descendant, Lord Byron, his description of the shipwreck in "Don Juan," is buried in the churchyard. Sir Francis Chantrey, the sculptor, was married at Twickenham Church in November, 1809, and Tennyson's son Hallam was baptised in 1852.

"Pope's Villa" is situated on the outskirts of Twickenham, in front of the road to Teddington, with a garden at the back looking towards the river. He became the possessor of it in 1718; and for thirty years the embellishment of its grounds was the favourite occupation of his leisure. The principal garden lay across the Teddington road; and to obtain easy access to it, the poet constructed a tunnel, which, when decorated with spars and shells, he called "a grotto," and celebrated both in prose and verse. "It contains," he says, "a spring of clearest water, which falls in a perpetual

---

[a] Robert Devereux, Earl of Essex; [b] Lord Clarendon; [c] the notorious Duke of Wharton; [d] Lady Mary Wortley Montague; [e] Henry Fielding, the novelist; [f] Henrietta, Countess of Suffolk; [g] Lady Fanny Shirley.

rill, that echoes through the cavern night and day. From the river Thames you see through my arch up a walk of the wilderness to a kind of open Temple, wholly composed of shells in the rustic manner; and from that distance, under the temple, you look down through a sloping arcade of trees, and see the sails on the river passing suddenly, and vanishing as through a perspective glass. When you shut the door of this grotto, it becomes on the instant, from a luminous room, a camera-obscura; on the wall of which all the objects on the river, hills, woods, and boats, are forming a moving picture in their visible radiations; and when you have a mind to light it up, it affords you a very different scene; it is finished with shells, interspersed with pieces of looking-glass in angular forms; and in the ceiling is a star of the same material, at which, when a lamp of an orbicular figure, of thin alabaster, is hung in the middle, a thousand pointed rays glitter, and are reflected over the place. There are connected to this grotto, by a narrower passage, two porches—one towards the river, of smooth stones, full of light, and open; the other toward the garden, shadowed with trees, and rough with shells, flints, and iron ore. The bottom is paved with simple pebble, as is also the adjoining walk up the wilderness to the temple, in the natural taste, agreeing not ill with the little dripping murmur and the aquatic idea of the whole place." In 1807, the villa passed into the hands of the Baroness Howe, who was Vandal enough to destroy it, and sweep away nearly every vestige of the poet's fanciful creations.

At Holyrood (then Chapel) House resided the poet Tennyson for a few months (1850-1852), previous to his removal to Freshwater, in the Isle of Wight.

On the north side of the church stands the Manor House, where Samuel Scott, the artist, at one time lived. It occupies the site of an older mansion, traditionally reputed to have belonged to Queen Katherine of Aragon. Orleans House, described by Defoe as "more properly a plantation, being in the middle betwixt the pasture, the kitchen garden, the fruit garden, and pleasure garden and wilderness," was rented by Louis Philippe, Duke of Orleans, for himself and brothers, from 1800 to 1807. Exiled again in 1815, he returned to Twickenham, and continued there until recalled to France in 1817. A third time it was his misfortune to become an exile, and despairing of ever recovering the French throne, he purchased Orleans House in 1852 for his son, the Duc d'Aumale, while he himself, through the Queen's courtesy, resided at Claremont. For some years Twickenham formed the Orleans head-quarters; the Prince de Joinville living at Mount Lebanon, the Comte de Paris at York House, and the Duc de Nemours at Bushey Park. In 1876 Orleans House was selected as the residence of Don Carlos of Spain.

At Twickenham Park resided the great Bacon for several years, until his pecuniary needs, about 1597, compelled him to sell it. After being connected with many distinguished names, it was divided into lots and sold in 1805. It is now covered with "genteel villas." Meadowbank is the residence of George Bishop, Esq., whose private observatory is under the direction of Mr. J. Russell Hind. Marble Hill was built by George II. for Mrs. Howard, Countess of Suffolk; at Little Marble Hill resided the charming actress, Mrs. Kitty Clive. It was afterwards called Spencer Grove, and tenanted by Lady Diana Beauclerk. "The laughter-loving dame," Mrs. Clive, removed to Little Strawberry Hill (on the lower road to Teddington), where she died in 1785. The Misses Berry afterwards became its tenants, and gave there, year after year, the most delightful afternoon reunions, at which might be seen everybody of distinction in the world of fashion or letters. Saville House was formerly the abode of the brilliant Lady Mary Wortley Montague; Twickenham House, of Sir John Hawkins, the friend of Johnson, and author of a "History of Music." Paul Whitehead, the satirist, lived at Colne Lodge; Turner, the great English landscape painter, at Sandycombe; Charles Dickens, at Ailsa Park.

A short walk inland, up a gentle ascent, leads to Strawberry Hill, where Horace Walpole, in 1747, erected his pseudo-Gothic "show-house," and collected all kinds of curiosities and articles of vertu, from Roman pottery and Damascus swords down to Sèvres china and Parisian

KINGSTON CHURCH AND BRIDGE.

snuff-boxes. The place may be regarded with some respect in spite of its pinchbeck, as the home of the author of the first English melodramatic romance, "The Castle of Otranto," and the most amusing, ingenious, and cold-blooded of letter-writers. It is now the seat of the Countess Waldegrave, who has restored as nearly as possible its original character, and laid out the grounds with admirable taste.

The Middlesex side of the river is lined with handsome houses and fair gardens up to and beyond Teddington (or Totyngton, an old settlement of the Totingas), where the first "weir" on the Thames occurs, and the influence of the ocean-tide ceases to be felt. Teddington Church is not an architecturally-remarkable building; but it is pleasantly situated, and contains, among other memorials, one to that most fascinating of actresses, "Peg Woffington." The Surrey bank exhibits a long stretch of low and level meadows, teeming with rich herbage, and bordered with a fringe of reeds and aquatic plants.

Kingston is one of the oldest towns in England, as it is one of the most agreeably situated. It possesses a kind of double existence; for while a large portion of it is occupied by traders and small shopkeepers, another is in the possession of the well-to-do, whose garden-girdled villas stretch along the slopes of a considerable hill, and form at Norbiton (North Barton) quite a settlement in themselves. One long street stretches through the lower part of the town from north to south, running parallel to the river, and continuing the main road from Richmond to Esher. This is intersected almost midway by the road from Wandsworth to Wimbledon, which crosses the river at Kingston Bridge—a handsome structure of stone, with seven arches, 386 feet long, built in 1825-1828. In an open space on the west side of the thoroughfare is situated the Town Hall, and just beyond it stands the grey old parish church. Through the outskirts of the town a road crosses the opulent and well-built suburb of Surbiton (South Barton) to the railway station, and thence proceeds, by way of Talworth, to Ewell and Reigate. On the opposite bank of the Thames, in deep shadow, repose the masses of foliage of Bushey Park, and the quaint old pile of Hampton Court is visible beyond them. The river-course is here diversified by several small aits, or islets, blooming with verdure.

From this brief sketch the reader will conclude, and rightly, that Kingston is as attractive a town as one can wish to live in, and, in fact, it is not only pleasant in itself, but in its surroundings. It commands some of the most charming views imaginable of wood and water, extending from the sequestered shades of Esher to the sunny uplands of Wimbledon and Putney. Wherever the river enters into the prospect, the spectator cannot be other than delighted and surprised; but even inland the pictures are full of variety and colour. They include broad-stretching vales, low and rolling hills, with masses of woodland; there are villas and farm-houses, green lanes and open heaths. The stranger will hardly believe in the number of admirable excursions that can be made around Kingston, or in the infinite variety of the scenery into which they will conduct him. He will hardly believe that almost within hearing of the roar of the Great Metropolis may be found the most picturesque solitudes, where the wanderer may idle through a summer's day in sweet companionship with birds and flowers.

We have spoken of Kingston as an ancient town, and there seems little doubt that it was of Roman origin. In early English times it was the scene of the coronation of several kings—Edward the Elder, 900; Æthelstan, 924; Eadmund, 940; Eadred, 946; Eadwig, 955; Eadgar, 959; Edward the Martyr, 975; Ethelred II., 978; Edmund II., 1016. In Domesday Book reference is made to it under its present name. It was frequently visited by King John, and at Surbiton are shown some fragments of an old building, absurdly called "King John's Dairy." In the struggle between the Barons, under Simon de Montfort, and Henry III., it seems to have sided with the popular hero. When Sir Thomas Wyatt broke out into rebellion against Queen Mary, in 1554, he advanced upon London by way of Kingston. He found the bridge broken, and some thirty feet of it carried clean away, while the Middlesex end was guarded by two hundred men. With an alert spirit, however, he directed a couple of pieces of ordnance to be directed against this small garrison, and quickly scattered it abroad. Whereupon he caused certain sailors to swim across the river, and loosen the barges which were moored to the opposite bank; and these being brought over, he and his partisans soon effected the passage.

ESHER CHURCH.

It is a curious coincidence that the great Civil War began and ended at Kingston. In January, 1641–2, Colonel Lemsford, Lord Digby, and a body of cavaliers sought to seize upon its magazine of arms, but were foiled by the vigilance of the Parliament. On the 1st of July, 1648, "in the lane between Kingston and Surbiton Common, was slain the beautiful [Lord] Francis Villiers, at an elm in the hedge of the east side of the lane, where, his horse being killed under him, he turned his back to the elm, and fought most valiantly with half-a-dozen. The enemy, coming on the other side of the hedge, pushed off his helmet, and killed him. On this elm was cut an ill-shaped 'V,' for Villiers, in memory of him." Francis was younger brother of the second Duke of Buckingham (Dryden's "Zimri"), who was present at the skirmish.

Such are the principal historic associations connected with Kingston. Its churches—the spacious parish church, of which the interior was restored in 1862, contains nine good brasses, and a monument to the Countess of Liverpool by Chantrey—and public buildings are numerous and excellent, but do not seem to call for detailed notice. It should be stated, however, that the Free Grammar School, established by Queen Elizabeth, can boast of having numbered Gibbon, the historian, among its pupils.

Resuming our river explorations, we leave the leafy shades of Bushey on our left, and on our right a succession of open meadows, broken up by hedges, and dotted with fine old trees. At Thames Ditton we come to a place pretty in itself, and interesting as the resort of several generations of anglers. Between Kingston and Hampton Bridge, be it observed, the stream is crowded with Izaak Walton's disciples, some perched in stationary punts, some seated in shady nooks on the banks, others standing knee-deep in the cool waters at such points as appear likely to reward their patient skill. Many of them, we may be sure, have sallied forth from the "Swan" at Ditton. Close to that time-honoured hostelry stands the picturesque mansion of Boyle Farm, the residence of the late distinguished lawyer, Lord St. Leonards.

About two miles inland lies the agreeable village of Esher, surrounded by groves, gardens, and meadows. Here, on the banks of the winding river, when the manor belonged to the see of Winchester, Bishop William of Waynflete erected a stately palace; the massive gate-house of which is still extant, but known, erroneously, as "Wolsey's Tower." It owes this name, in all probability, to the circumstance that the great Cardinal resided at the palace for three or four weeks after his sudden downfall in 1529. He and his retainers were "without either beds, sheets, table-clothes, dishes to eat their meat in, or wherewithal to buy any: howbeit, there was good provision of all kinds of victual, and of beer and wine, whereof there was sufficient and plenty enough." The other articles Wolsey was compelled to borrow of the Bishop of Carlisle and Master Arundell. His illness compelled him to leave Esher for Richmond early in 1550.

Esher afterwards passed to the famous admiral, Lord Howard of Effingham, and, at a later period, to the great Anglo-Indian statesman, Lord Clive. In the old churchyard lies the dust of Anna Maria Porter, the novelist, whose "Thaddeus of Warsaw" was almost as widely read by her generation as "Daniel Deronda" is by our own. What a wide gulf, however, between Anna Maria Porter and George Eliot! And what a contrast between the literary taste which idolised the former, and the intellectual appreciation which commends the latter! Esher House is a "seat" of some pretensions, which at one time belonged to Harry Pelham, the chief minister of George II., and brother to the Duke of Newcastle. The grounds are rich in picturesque effects; hills and dales are clothed with thriving woods; nor is the beauty of flowing water wanting. The so-called "Wolsey's Tower" forms a striking feature in the landscape.

WOLSEY'S TOWER.

Adjoining Esher lies the royal manor of Claremont. Sir John Vanbrugh, dramatist and architect, built a house here in Queen Anne's reign, which, in 1715, he sold to the Duke of Newcastle. The Duke greatly enlarged the mansion, and employed Kent, the landscape gardener, to lay out and beautify the grounds. He it was who named the place "Clare-mont," from his earldom of Clare. It afterwards passed into the hands of Lord Clive, who remodelled the grounds under the superintendence of "Capability" Brown, and erected a new mansion at an immense cost. This was in the season of Clive's unpopularity, when he was commonly looked upon as an incarnation of all the vices; as an adventurer who had wrung his wealth by blood and torture from the wretched princes of India. "Brown, whom," says Macaulay, "Clive employed to lay out his pleasure-grounds, was amazed to see in the house of his noble employer a chest which had once been filled with gold from the treasury of Moorshedabad, and could not understand how the conscience of the criminal could suffer him to sleep with such an object so near to his bedchamber. The peasantry of Surrey looked with mysterious horror on the stately house which was rising at Claremont, and whispered that the great wicked lord had ordered the walls to be made so thick in order to keep out the devil, who would one day carry him away bodily." The undeserved obloquy in which he was involved, and the colossal ingratitude with which his great services were treated, so worked on a mind perturbed by disease, that the unfortunate statesman committed suicide, on the 22nd of November, 1774.

Claremont, many years afterwards, was purchased by the Crown, and settled on the Princess Charlotte and her husband, Leopold of Saxe-Coburg. The Princess died here, in childbirth, to the intense grief of the nation, on the 6th of November, 1807. Brighter memories are now connected with it through the occasional residence of the Queen and the Prince Consort, and (for some months after their marriage) of the Princess Louise and the Marquis of Lorne; while the Duke of Connaught and his bride spent their honeymoon here in 1879. We may add that Louis Philippe, ex-King of the French, died at Claremont in 1850. The house is a solid-looking quadrangular pile, to which a fine Corinthian portico lends a certain dignity of character. The grounds are beautifully varied, and within a circuit of three and a-half miles present a rich succession of striking landscapes, some wild and sylvan, some graceful and picturesque, and some endowed with a quiet pastoral beauty. There is also a fine lake, with a wooded island in the centre.

CLAREMONT.

HAMPTON COURT PALACE

ENTRANCE TO HAMPTON COURT PALACE.

CHAPTER IV.

HAMPTON COURT.

ROSSING Hampton Bridge, and pausing to admire the beautiful view of the river, with its wooded eyots, which it commands, we duly arrive at the main entrance to Hampton Court Palace. Away to the left stretches the Green, where, in the days of the Tudors and the Stuarts, much "tilting" was carried on; and where, in the days of Victoria, London citizens and their families disport themselves according to the "sad" English fashion. In front of us, beyond a range of well-built houses, rise the green tops of the chestnuts and hawthorns of Bushey Park. It is needless to say that all round about the hanging signs proclaim an abundance of "entertainment for man and horse." The inn known as the "the Toy" perpetuates the name (corrupted from the *tois* or *toils*, the network barriers used in the tilting-games), but does not occupy the site, of the ancient hostelry, where William "the Deliverer" was accustomed to entertain his cavaliers with dinners of rump-steak, washed down by Dutch "schnapps," and enveloped in clouds of fragrant tobacco smoke.

THE PALACE ERECTED BY WOLSEY.

A solid wall of red brick separates the Palace-grounds from the Green; and in front of this wall runs a broad walk, lined by elm and chestnut, which Queen Mary and her maids of honour much frequented. Their constant resorting to it led to its being popularly known as the *Frau*—since strangely corrupted into *Frog*—walk. The Palace entrance is duly distinguished by the royal arms. To the right extends a range of offices, and, opposite, the long line of the cavalry barracks, with the usual appurtenances. Both are wholly unworthy of their situation, and absolutely degrade the approach to the Palace. The contrast which they present to the well-proportioned gateway tower, erected by Wolsey, is at once startling and suggestive.

The manor of Hampton formerly belonged to the Knights Hospitallers of St. John of Jerusalem, from whom it was leased by Cardinal Wolsey, for the purpose of erecting on the site of the old manor-house a palace worthy of his fortunes. In 1515 he began to realise his design, and with such vigour and energy did he push forward the works that he was soon able to take up his residence there. The plan was conceived on a magnificent scale, and the details were all in keeping with it. In truth, the splendour of the new building, and the sumptuous state which the great Cardinal maintained in it, soon awakened the jealousy of Henry VIII., and Wolsey found it advisable to propitiate his royal master by presenting him with the Palace and all it contained. The gift was immediately accepted, and in acknowledgment of it Henry licensed the Cardinal to occupy the Royal Palace at Richmond whenever he pleased, and occasionally permitted him to retire to Hampton Court itself.

The King made large additions to the Palace—"till it became more like a city than a house;" and these (especially the Great Hall) were conceived in a spirit not inferior to Wolsey's. To secure the necessary seclusion, as well as entertainment, he cleared the surrounding country of inhabitants and stocked it with deer, extending the "Honour," or demesne, for miles around, so that it included Cobham, Weybridge, Byfleet, the two Moleseys, Esher, and Ditton. He appears to have been very partial to this beautiful river-side retreat. It was here that he received the intelligence of Wolsey's death. Here, in 1531, Anne Boleyn, as Queen, was the central figure in every revel, banquet, and pastime. Queen Jane Seymour died here, shortly after giving birth to Edward VI. (1537). The young Prince was brought up at Hampton with a vast degree of care. "It was commanded," says Froude, "that no person, of what rank soever, except the regular attendants in the nursery, should approach the cradle without an order under the King's hand. The food supplied for the child's use was to be largely 'assayed.' His clothes were to be washed by his own servants, and no other hand might touch them. The material was to be submitted to all tests of poison. The chamberlain or vice-chamberlain must be present, morning and evening, when the Prince was washed and dressed; and nothing of any kind, bought for the use of the nursery, might be introduced till it had been aired and perfumed. No person—not even the domestics of the palace—might have access to the Prince's rooms, except those who were specially appointed to them; nor might any member of the household approach London during the unhealthy season, for fear of their catching and conveying infection." Here, on July 2nd, 1543, Catherine Parr was married and proclaimed Queen; and here, at one of Henry's gorgeous festivals, the poet-Earl of Surrey first saw, and loved, his Geraldine:—

"Hampton me taught to wish her first for mine."

After Henry's death, the country folk petitioned the King's Council for relief; and the Lord Protector Somerset ordered the Honour to be "dechased," the deer to be killed or removed, and the land restored at the old rents to the old tenants.

Edward VI. frequently resided at Hampton Court. He was here in the late autumn of 1549, when his uncle, the Protector, informed the Council of the confederacy formed against himself under the leadership of the Earl of Warwick, and a hurried proclamation was issued, requiring all the King's loving subjects "to repair to his Highness at his Majesty's manor of Hampton Court, in most defensible array, with banners and weapons, to defend his most royal person and his most entirely beloved uncle, the Lord Protector, against whom certain had attempted a most dangerous conspiracy." But the wheel of fortune swung round; Somerset fell; and at Hampton Court, in 1551, Edward created the Earl of Warwick Duke of Northumberland. Queen Mary retired hither with her Spanish husband soon after their marriage, living in a seclusion that deepened the popular repugnance to the alliance. Here she received her sister, the Princess Elizabeth, and her confessors endeavoured to persecute the Princess into an abjuration of Protestantism. Elizabeth owed her life, apparently, to King Philip's good offices; and in the Christmas festivities at the Palace in 1544, still through his good offices, she occupied her proper place—"The Princess supped at the same table with the King and Queen, next the cloth of state; and after supper, was served with a perfumed napkin and plates of confects by the Lord Paget." We also read:—"On St. Stephen's Day she heard matins in the Queen's closet adjoining to the chapel, where she was attired in a robe of white satin, strung all over with large pearls. On the 29th day of December, she sate with their Majesties and the nobility at a grand spectacle of jousting, when 200 spears were broken. Half of the combatants were accoutred in the Almaine, and half in the Spanish fashion." When Elizabeth became Queen she frequently visited Hampton Court, and it was beneath its roof she discussed with her lords the charge against Mary, Queen of Scots, of having conspired with Bothwell to murder Henry Darnley. It was here, on the 4th of December, 1568, the Regent Murray produced the fatal casket. "The entire evidence was placed in the hands of the Council. . . . The casket was opened, and the letters, presents, and contracts were taken out and read. They were examined long and minutely by each and every of the lords who were present," and declared genuine. Here it was, in 1604, that James I. held the famous "Conference" of prelates and Puritan divines, for the discussion of the grievances alleged by the latter; a conference in which he made great display of his own theological learning, and when the Puritans ventured to dispute his conclusions, hastily threatened that he would make them conform, or would harry them out of the land.

The brightest hours of the chequered life of Charles I.—those which he spent in the bosom of his family and the indulgence of his refined tastes—were passed at Hampton Court. Here he received the Ambassadors of France and Denmark, in July, 1625; here he knighted, in October, 1638, Balthazar Gerbier, the painter; hither, in January, 1642, he and his Queen retired from the insurrection in London, excited by his abortive attempt to arrest "the Five Members." In August, 1647, he came to Hampton as a prisoner, and remained for three months under gentle supervision, carrying on negotiations with Cromwell and the Army which he never meant to bring to any definite issue. Lady Fanshawe visited him here —"I went three times," she says, "to pay my duty to his Majesty, both as I was the daughter of his servant and the wife of his servant. The last time I ever saw him I could not refrain from weeping. He kissed me when we took our leave of him; and I, with streaming eyes, prayed aloud to God to preserve his Majesty with a long and happy life. The King patted me on the cheek, and said, impressively, 'Child, if God willest, it shall be so; but you and I must submit to God's will, and you know what hands I am in.' Then, turning to my husband, Sir Richard Fanshawe, he said, 'Be sure, Dick, to tell my son all I have said, and deliver these letters to my wife. I pray God to bless her, and preserve her, and all will be well.' Then taking my husband in his arms, he said, 'Thou hast ever been an honest man! I hope God will bless thee, and make thee a happy servant to my son.' Thus did we part from that benign light, which was extinguished soon after, to the grief of all Christians not forsaken of their God." Charles escaped from the Court on the night of the 11th of November, 1647, a night as dark and stormy as his fortunes, and made his way to the Hampshire coast, and so to Carisbrook Castle, in the Isle of Wight; a strange error, which threw him completely into the hands of his sternest opponents. In 1656 the Palace was purchased by Cromwell, with whom, during the brief remainder of his life, it became a favourite residence. Here his daughter Elizabeth was wedded to Lord Falconbridge, November 18, 1657; here he lost his well-loved daughter, Lady Claypole, August 6th, 1658; and here, a fortnight later, he was seized with the fever of which she died. "I met him," says George Fox, the Quaker, "riding into Hampton Court Park; and before I came to him, as he rode at the head of his lifeguard, I saw and felt a waft of death go forth against him." Harvey, his Groom of the Bedchamber, writes, "At Hampton Court, a few days after the death of the Lady Elizabeth, which touched him nearly," his Highness was "himself under bodily distempers, forerunners of that sickness which was to death." On the 20th of August he was better: but next day, Saturday, a great change took place, and symptoms of tertian ague were observed. He returned to Whitehall on the following Tuesday, and on the 3rd of September passed away.

The Palace was not held in less esteem by Charles II., of whose diversions here the gossiping pages of Pepys, who walked from Teddington to see "the noble furniture and splendid pictures," and the *Chronique Scandaleuse* of Count Grammont, afford some glimpses. Evelyn has left on record a graphic description of the Palace as it was in the summer of 1662:—"It is as noble and uniform a pile, and as capacious, as any Gothic architecture can have made it. There is incomparable furniture in it, especially hangings designed by Raphael, very rich with gold; also many rare pictures, especially the 'Cæsarian Triumphs' of Andr. Mantegna, formerly the Duke of Mantua's. Of the tapestries, I believe the world can show nothing nobler of the kind than the stories of Abraham and Tobit. The gallery of horns is very particular for the vast beams of stags, elks, antelopes, etc. The Queen's Bed was an embroidery of silver on crimson velvet, and cost £8000, being a present made by the States of Holland when his Majesty returned, and had formerly been given by them to our King's sister, the Princess of Orange, and, being bought of her again, was now presented to the King. The great looking-glass and toilet, of beaten and massive gold, was given by the Queen-mother. The Queen brought over with her from Portugal such Indian cabinets as had never before been seen here. The Great Hall is a most magnificent room; the chapel roof excellently fretted and gilt. I was also curious to visit the wardrobes and tents, and other furniture of state; the park, forming a flat naked piece of ground, and planted with sweet rows of lime trees; and the canal for water, now near perfected; also the hare park. In the garden is a rich and noble fountain, with syrens, statues, etc., cast in copper by Favelli, but no plenty of water. The cradle-walk of hornbeam in the garden is, for the perplexed twining of the trees, very observable."

A not less glowing picture than this is drawn by Catherine of Braganza's Portuguese historian, who also describes the balls and revels, and the river pageants, and the open-air pastimes that made the Palace gay. It was the English "home" of William III., who nowhere else in England could reproduce so nearly the conditions of his court on the Hague. He loved the placid flow of the broad river; the murmur of the reeds and sedges that lined its banks; the pleasant formality of the level gardens that extended in front of the Palace; the shade of elm and chestnut, arranged in leafy groups or noble avenues. Here he built and planted; the Maze, the Wilderness, and the Gardens were laid out by his direction. Here, too, on the 20th of February, 1702, while he was riding in the Park, his favourite horse, Sorrel, struck his foot against a mole-hill, and, stumbling, threw his rider. On taking him up, his attendants found that he had broken his collar bone, and he was removed to Kensington—to die. Queen Anne was not less partial to the court than her predecessor;[*] and its state as a royal palace was fully maintained by the First and Second Georges. Then its glory began to decay. The Third George affected Kew, and the Fourth George restored Windsor Castle. So it came to pass that the fierce light which beats upon a throne ceased to illuminate Hampton Court; and while the Hall and State apartments were thrown open

---

[*] "Here thou, great Anna! whom these realms obey,
Dost sometimes counsel take—and sometimes tea;
Hither the lovers and the nymphs resort,
To taste awhile the pleasures of a Court."—POPE.

freely for public inspection, the other portions were formed into residences at the disposal of the Sovereign, which are usually allotted to the widows and families of military officers of high repute but narrow means.

Of the five quadrangles which originally composed the Palace only three remain. The third, or Fountain Court, was built by Sir Christopher Wren for William III., but exhibits few signs of his great architectural genius. Perhaps he was cramped by that lack of funds of which Queen Mary complains in a letter to her royal consort:—"I hear of so much use for money, and find so little, that I cannot tell whether that of Hampton Court will not be the worst for it." During the work of reconstruction the King and Queen resided in "the Water Gallery," a portion of which, the banqueting-room, is still in existence. The original character of the first, or Outer Court, and the second, or Clock Court,* has not been seriously modified; though the pseudo-classic additions to the second Court and to Henry VIII.'s Hall are not improvements. Some years ago the Great Hall † was carefully restored, and alcoved windows, "blushing with scutcheons," were introduced, from designs by Willement. Few nobler apartments are to be found in England. The harmony of the proportions, the majestic sweep of the lofty open roof, the general air of grandeur and dignity, combined with the pomp of banners, and the rich hangings of ancient tapestry, and the gleaming groups of armour, produce a powerful effect on the imagination. It is like a chapter taken out of an old chronicle and set bodily before us. It recalls the pageantry and chivalrous circumstances of the past—its brightest and most picturesque side—as nothing else can. At once we people it with the men and women of the old time—with Henry VIII. and his courtiers, or with Charles I. and his family; or we see the great Lord Protector pacing it slowly, with his mind intent upon the grave concerns of the nation he ruled with so strong a hand. It furnishes a vivid commentary upon English history, when we remember how many generations of our Kings have fluttered through their brief day of splendour beneath this stately roof.

Hawthorne, the American novelist, describes the Hall as "a most noble and beautiful room, about a hundred feet long, and sixty high and broad. Most of the windows," he adds, "are of stained or painted glass, with elaborate designs. The walls, from the floor to perhaps half their height, are covered with antique tapestry, which, though a good deal faded, still retains colour enough to be a very effective ornament, and to give an idea of how rich a mode of decking a noble apartment this must have been. The subjects represented were from Scripture, and the figures seemed natural. On looking closely at this tapestry, you would see that it was thickly interwoven with threads of gold, still glistening. The windows, except one or two that are long, do not descend below the top of this tapestry, and are, therefore, twenty or thirty feet above the floor;

---

* The Fountain Court measures 110 feet by 167; the Western, or Outer Court, 167 feet by 161; and the Middle, or Clock Court, 133 feet by 92 feet.

† It measures 106 feet long, 40 feet wide, and 60 feet high.

and this manner of lighting a great room seems to add much to the impressiveness of the enclosed space. The roof is very magnificent, of carved oak, intricately and elaborately arched, and still as perfect to all appearance as when it was first made. There are banners—so fresh in their hues, and so untattered, that I think they must be modern—suspended along beneath the cornice of the Hall, and exhibiting Wolsey's arms and badges. On the whole, this is a perfect sight in its way."

The tapestry here is Flemish, and represents the history of Abraham, in eight compartments. That at the entrance is of earlier date, and of the school of Albert Durer; the subject, Justice and Mercy pleading before Kings. In the withdrawing-room, which measures seventy feet long by twenty-five feet high, the tapestry is covered with mythological designs. This apartment contains some cartoons of Carlo Cignani, and a marble statue of Venus.

By the King's Staircase, over the walls and ceilings of which sprawl Verrio's unmeaning allegories, we ascend to the apparently interminable suite of the State Apartments. These are mainly wainscoted with oak, dating from William III.'s reign. Around the panels and over many of the doorways may be seen some of that wonderful wood-carving by Grinling Gibbons, in which fruit, and foliage, and wreaths of flowers are represented with a delicacy and an exactness that have never been surpassed. The apartments open one beyond another in a succession apparently as interminable as the line of Banquo, so that to traverse the whole of them is almost a day's journey, and leaves a confused and bewildering impression on the mind. There are King's drawing-rooms and Queen's drawing-rooms, King's bedchambers and Queen's bedchambers, King's closets and Queen's closets, besides audience-chambers and the like. We have no space to enumerate the pictures with which every wall is covered; pictures good, bad, and indifferent. In Italian canvases the collection is specially rich, but there are good specimens of every school. It is to be regretted that they are not arranged on some intelligible principle, and in such a way as to contribute to the art-education of the thousands who visit the Palace.

Almost every room has some article of upholstery of the time of William, Anne, or George—such as Queen Anne's State Bed, and William and Mary's, which is worth a more or less cursory glance—and each commands from its windows a fine view of the gardens, sparkling with flowers and fountains, of the broad calm river, and the green Surrey hills beyond. "It is one of the pleasantest things in a visit here," says Thorne, "to sit awhile, if the room be not crowded, in one of these window-seats, and let the eye, which is growing fatigued with dwelling so long on the gaud and glitter of art, refresh itself by resting on the soft verdure and gentle features of nature."

Let us now pass into the Gardens. They are of considerable size, and admirably kept. In Queen Elizabeth's time, Hentzner describes them as being "most pleasant." In Charles II.'s they were laid out anew by the royal gardener, Rose, in the then popular French taste; but their present arrangement is mainly due to the Dutch proclivities of

William III., who employed Loudon and Wise to carry out his designs. We confess that to us there is something very agreeable in their trim preciseness. It preserves the old-world character of the scene, and harmonises fitly with the quaint attitude of the Palace itself. It seems impossible not to be delighted by the long lines of noble trees, the broad straight walks, the "pleached alleys," the glossy bowers, the soft smooth lawns, the shining columns of leaping water, and the parterres brimming over with bright colour. The garden-front of the palace is Wren's, and when viewed in connection with the walks and terraces becomes respectable. Opposite to its very centre is situated a fountain, with a large circular basin, in which gold and silver fish display their glancing hues; this is a good point from which to obtain a general view of the Palace and Gardens.

The Gardens extend from Bushey Park to the river. Also extending to the river, and in front of the Palace, lies the Home Park, where the artist's eye will find pleasure in some noble trees. The private garden is not less worth a visit. Observe, on the left, the quaint old pleasaunce, sole relic of the Elizabethan mansion-house; it forms a rectangular oblong, and glows with the poets' old-fashioned flowers—with rose, and clove, and pink, and stock, and lavender—just as it did when the Knights Hospitallers sunned themselves on its terraces. Observe, too, the glossy hedge of evergreen which fences this lovely walk from the bitter East. A never-failing attraction to visitors is the Vinery, with the well-known "vine," a Black Hamburg, which covers a surface of 110 feet or more, and has grown no fewer than 1750 splendid bunches of grapes in a season. It was planted in 1769; its stem is 30 inches in circumference. The average yearly produce is 1500 bunches. Reference must finally be made to the Wilderness, which is closely set with magnificent trees; and to the Maze, an evergreen labyrinth, situated at the farther extremity.

Surely this brief sketch is sufficient to extort from the reader some such admission as that of Hawthorne's:—"What a noble palace, nobly enriched, is this Hampton Court!" The American continues:—"The English Government does well to keep it up, and to admit the public freely into it for it is impossible for even a Republican not to feel something like awe—at least, a profound respect—for all this state, and for the institutions which are here represented; the Sovereigns, whose usual magnificence demands such a residence; and its permanence, too, enduring from age to age, and each royal generation adding new splendours to those accumulated by their predecessors."

Leaving by the Lion Gate, we cross the road into Bushey Park, a beautiful sylvan demesne, finely planted with grand old trees, the trunks of which are grown with moss, and traversed from end to end by William III.'s chestnut avenue—a thing of glory, unequalled and indescribable in its season of bloom. The Park is said to take its name from its abundance of hawthorn. It is at all times of the year a place to see and admire; but it wears its chief splendour in that delightful period—half-May, half-June—

"Half-prankt with spring, with summer half-imbrown'd,"

LONG WALK, WINDSOR PARK

when its hawthorns are alive with flowers, and its limes load the air with fragrance, and its mile-long avenue (planted by William III.) of horse-chestnuts breaks into flowery pyramids. A sight to enjoy and to remember is the mass of pink and white blossom clustered on either side of the drive, which, on "Show Sunday," or "Chestnut Sunday," rivals Hyde Park, in the "season," with its almost interminable procession of carriages. He who then visits Bushey Park will enjoy an intellectual feast as great as if he were suddenly transferred to

"Boccaccio's garden and its faëry,
The love, the joyaunce, and the gallantry;"

and taking it in connection with "royal Hampton's pile," will feel constrained to admit that a day thus spent deserves henceforth to be marked with a white stone; to be included among those few memorable days of which the mind desires to preserve the recollection until the very last.

ANCIENT SUN-DIAL AT HAMPTON COURT.

CHAPTER V.

MOLESEY—HAMPTON—WALTON—WEYBRIDGE—OATLANDS.

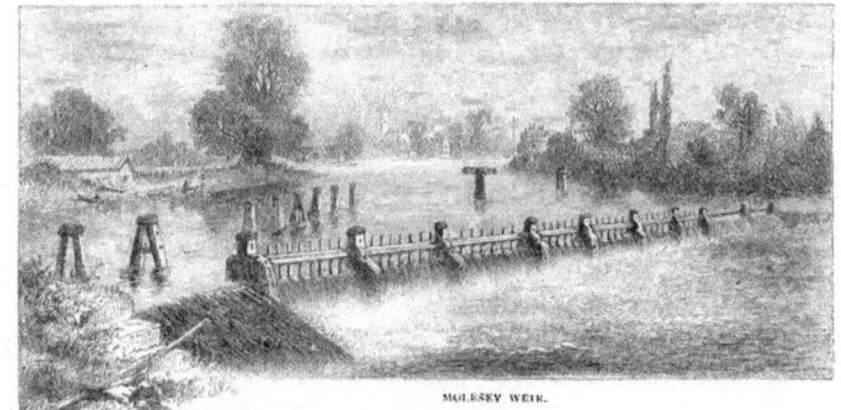

MOLESEY WEIR.

L EAVING behind us Hampton Court, in the shadow of its past glories, we pass through Molesey Lock, in continuance of our upward river voyage. On our right the trim villa residences of Hampton, with their well-ordered gardens, line the banks, until they gradually merge into the charming village of Sunbury. Conspicuous objects as we glide along are the bizarre-looking water-towers of the London Water Companies, whose architects do not seem to have succeeded in combining utility with beauty. The most noticeable "lion" in Hampton is Garrick Villa (formerly called Hampton House), situated a little to the right of the Church. It was occupied by the great actor from 1754 till his death in 1779, and afterwards by his widow, till her death in 1822. Its external appearance has undergone but little change; the handsome classical façade, added by Garrick in 1755, was designed by Adam, one of the brother-architects who erected the Adelphi Buildings in London. On the lawn, Garrick raised an octagonal Grecian temple for the reception of Roubiliac's statue of Shakespeare, now in the entrance hall of the British Museum.

SUNBURY AND WALTON.

The river at this point presents a chain of eyots of picturesque appearance. Anglers may be reminded that it is rigidly "preserved" along what is known as Hampton Deep —a stretch of 960 yards, from Garrick Villa to the Tumbling Bay. The streamlets and ponds on the Surrey side are the scene of the operations of the Thames Angling Preservation Society, which breeds and rears fish on a tolerably extensive scale. It has also several rearing-ponds at Sunbury.

Sunbury Church is a curious edifice, both externally and internally. Artist and architect have freely indulged their freaks of fancy in its construction and decoration. The delightfulest thing about it is its peal of bells, which rings melodiously in the rower's ear as he propels his skiff through the summer twilight, or tarries till he can effect his passage through Sunbury Lock. The river takes a sharp curve beyond, and brings us in front of the well-looking houses, with good old trees about them, which form the hamlet of Lower Halliford—the first place from the river's mouth, as Dr. Guest remarks, named after a ford across the Thames. The dwellers in Lower Halliford may be considered to have their lot cast in pleasant places. The situation is healthy and convenient; the scenery of a very agreeable character. The winding course of the shining river, which trails through the low rich pasture- lands like a ribbon of silver on "cloth of green," presents a succession of sweet pastoral views; while these are diversified by glimpses of Walton in one direction, and of Weybridge on the other, with the groves of Oatlands between them.

SUNBURY CHURCH.

But still pleasanter the lot of the inhabitant of Walton. He must be fit for "treasons, stratagems, and spoils," if he love not the broad green meadows that lie round about it, its long lines of stately trees, its copses rich in low-growing foliage, and above all, its exquisite river pictures, whether as seen in the ash-grey light of early morning, or as touched with gold and purple, when the sunset throws its broad level rays upon the piers and iron girders of Walton Bridge. The village, or rather town, runs up from the Thames in several irregular streets, which open out towards the gorse-golden expanse of Walton Common, or the richly wooded parks of Ashley, Burwood, and Oatlands. There are many good residences in the vicinity, and villas of more or less pretension are springing up at every vantage-point. Mount Felix, visible from the river, which it skirts with its grounds, was the seat of the late Earl of Tankerville, and built for him by Sir Charles Barry, in Sir Charles's favourite Italian style. It was afterwards the residence of Herbert Ingram, the founder of illustrated journalism. Its tower is 70 feet high. The park is finely laid out, and finely wooded. Here flourish lofty cedars; deodar, Chili, and silver pines; scarlet oaks, of vigorous growth; and purple beeches, which are truly things of beauty. On the right of the road to the railway stands the Elizabethan mansion of Ashley Park, which owes its present character to Richard Boyle, Lord Shannon, its possessor in the reign of the Second George. It is built in the form of an H, with gabled ends, which secure most striking effects of light and shade. The Great Hall occupies the entire height of the building; the Gallery is 100 feet in length. The grounds are splendidly wooded, and at several points they open up vistas of the most picturesque character. Another richly wooded demesne is that of Burwood Park, lying beyond the Common, and spreading its masses of foliage over four hundred acres. We have no space for detailed notice of Pain's Hill—an extensive estate near Cobham, the gardens of which were eulogised by Walpole and Gray—the Vicarage; Silvermere, with its gleaming lake; Burhill, and Burwood House; Brokenhurst, and the Manor House. Holme Lodge is the charming residence of the eminent painter, John F. Lewis.

The Church at Walton deserves and will repay a visit, not on account of its architectural features, but because its associations are exceptionally interesting. In the vestry you are shown a Scold's, or Gossip's Bridle, consisting of a thin circlet of iron, which passed over and round the head, so as to thrust into the mouth a small flat iron bit, two inches long by one broad, for the purpose of holding down a refractory tongue. The whole is made fast by a padlock. It was presented SCOLD'S BRIDLE. to the parish, in 1623, by a squire who had lost an estate "through the instrumentality of a lying, gossiping woman," and it bears the following inscription:—

"Chester presents Walton with a bridle
To curb women's tongues that talk too idle."

On a low pillar near the pulpit is deeply engraved the well-known verse with which Elizabeth, it is alleged, baffled the inquiries of a pertinacious theologian:—

"Christ was the Worde and spake it:
He took the Bread and brake it;
And what the Word doth make it,
That I believe and take it."

In the north aisle, observe Roubiliac's splendid monument to the second and last Viscount Shannon, a soldier of good repute. He is represented in a field-marshal's uniform, with cloak and baton; a lowered flag behind him, a military tent above him, and cannon, flags, and other military insignia on either side. The D'Oyley memorial, with its weeping female figure, came from the chisel of Chantrey.

By the altar lies a black marble slab inscribed to Jerome Weston, Earl of Portland, died 1662; and in front of the south entrance to the chancel a "fair black marble stone" records the death, in 1681, of William Lilly, the astrologer, who lived at Horsham, hard by, for sixteen years, and lives for ever in the pages of "Hudibras":—

> "Quoth Ralph, not far from hence doth dwell
> A cunning man, hight Sidrophel;
> That deals in Destiny's dark counsels,
> And sage Opinions of the Moon sells."

Enclosed in an oaken frame, and attached to the north wall of the chancel, are four small brasses, perpetuating the memory of John Selwyn, "Keeper of Her Ma'ties Parke of Otelande, under ye Right Honourable Charles Howward, Lord Admyral of England," died 1587—the year before Howard gained immortal fame by defeating the Armada —his wife, their five sons, and six daughters. One of the brasses exhibits him in his habit as he lived, with a horn slung to his belt; a second shows Mistress Selwyn in hat and ruff; a third, the figures of their eleven children; and a fourth refers to a tradition thus told by Grose. "He (Selwyn) was extremely famous for his strength, agility, and skill in horsemanship, specimens of which he exhibited before the Queen at a grand stag-hunt in the park (Oatlands); where, attending, as was the duty of his office, he, in the heat of the chace, suddenly leaped from his horse upon the back of the stag (both running at that time with their utmost speed), and not only kept his seat gracefully in spite of every effort of the affrightened beast, but, drawing his sword, with it guided him towards the Queen, and coming near her presence, plunged it into his throat, so that the animal fell dead at her feet. This was thought sufficiently wonderful to be chronicled on his monument, and he is accordingly there portrayed in the act of stabbing the beast."

Returning to the village, we come, in Church Street, on the old brick-and-timber house, now, unfortunately, much disfigured and dilapidated, which was occupied by Bradshaw, the President of the High Court of Justice that condemned Charles I. It is divided into several small tenements, but internally retains some of its original Jacobean characteristics. Tradition asserts that Charles's death-warrant was signed in a panelled chamber on the ground floor of the west wing. It was long believed that a subterranean passage extended from the house under the Thames, and that the spirit of the stern regicide roamed at night about the ancient ruins. At Walton was born that famous old sea-dog, Admiral Rodney, who introduced the effective naval manœuvre of "breaking the enemy's line," and whose victories over the Spanish fleet, under Don Juan de Langara, in 1780, and over the French, under the Comte de Grasse, in 1782, were among the most notable of British sea-fights in the pre-Nelson period. Dr. William Maginn, the wit and scholar, a popular contributor to "Fraser" and "Blackwood," died in a house opposite the Bear Inn, on the 20th of August, 1842, and is buried (without a memorial) in the churchyard.

Many of our readers will be familiar with Turner's fine picture of Walton Bridge. The picturesque structure which he portrayed with so much glory of colour has, however, been replaced by one of iron and brick, designed by Murray, and opened in 1863. This connects with the Surrey roadway by a second bridge, of fifteen low brick arches, which spans a meadow bottom, often inundated in winter. From the bridge and the ground above it, a view of the highest beauty is obtainable; sylvan and yet semi-pastoral in its elements; the river flowing between densely wooded banks, "the charm of this enchanted ground." Artist, amateur oarsman, angler, or tourist in search of the picturesque, or antiquary hunting up memorials of the past, will alike find abundant entertainment and occupation at Walton.

WALTON BRIDGE.

For the antiquary, indeed, the field is ample, whether he turn his steps to the numerous earthworks in the neighbourhood, or the Brito-Roman camp upon St. George's Hill (a wooded eminence, commanding prospects equally delightful and extensive), or the fortified ford known as Coway Stakes. This ford lies just above the bridge, and is now almost unanimously recognised by experts as the scene of Cæsar's passage of the Thames in pursuit of the Britons under Cassivellaunus. "The river," says the great Roman, "could be crossed on foot only at one place, and there with difficulty. When Cæsar reached this point, he found a large force drawn up on the opposite bank. The bank had also been defended by sharp stakes fixed in front, while similar stakes fixed under water were concealed by the stream. Cæsar, having learned these particulars from prisoners and deserters, sent forward his cavalry, and ordered the legions to follow immediately. But the soldiers went so swiftly, and with such a rush, that, though only their heads were above the water, the enemy, unable to withstand the onset, retired from the bank of the river and took to flight." In Bede's time (early in the 8th century) the stakes were still visible; as thick, he says, as a man's leg, encased with lead, and fixed immovably in the river-bed. Some of them existed as late as 1734, and even to the beginning of the present century. Of late years the channel of the river has been considerably deepened, and all traces of the ford have vanished. But the imaginative traveller will not find it difficult, as he looks on the calm river from the summit of Walton Bridge, to picture the glittering helmets and uplifted eagles of the Roman legionaries, as they broke through the rushing current; and in his ear will faintly echo the war-cries of the Britons as they sought to maintain their ground in the unequal fight.

Adjoining Walton, and stretching between the Thames and the Wey, lies Oatlands Park, a royal demesne, and the seat of a royal palace during the Tudor and Stuart periods. "A very fair building," says Aubrey, "and, when in its glory, much resorted to by the royal family, nobility, and gentry during the summer season." Brave sights have been seen at Oatlands! "In the park was once a paddock, with a Standing, where Queen Elizabeth was used to shoot with a cross-bow."* Queen Anne of Denmark reared

COWAY STAKES.

silkworms here, and magnificently entertained the Venetian Ambassador, Busano. Her son, Prince Henry, was born here in 1603. Oatlands was Henrietta Maria's dower-house, and the birthplace of the Duke of Gloucester. After the death of Charles I. the palace was dismantled and the park disparked; but something in the way of restoration was effected "when the King had his own again." In 1696, William III. granted it to Arthur Herbert, Earl of Torrington, who fought the great sea-fight off Beachy Head, in 1690, so graphically described by Macaulay. It afterwards passed into the hands of the Clintons, and a new mansion was built, in 1725, by the Earl of Lincoln, which was enlarged by that shuffling, shambling politician, his grandson, Henry Duke of Newcastle. He it was who constructed the great lake and the celebrated Grotto. The latter still remains. It is said that three Italians, a father and his sons, were employed upon it for several years. The exterior is composed of tufa; the interior, which is divided into five rooms or cells, shines with an infinite number of quaint devices wrought in spars, ores, shells, crystals, and stalactites. In the upper room, which has a cupola of stalactites, George IV., when Prince Regent, entertained at supper the Allied Sovereigns, with their princes and generals, on the occasion of their visit to England after the Battle of Waterloo. About 1790, Oatlands was purchased by the Duke of York, and the house having been partly destroyed by fire in 1794, a new house in the pseudo-Gothic style was built, and became the Duchess's favourite residence until she died in 1820. Curious sketches of the domestic interior of the Duke and Duchess, ranging over upwards

---

* A couple of yew trees, 60 yards apart, are still called "Queen Elizabeth's Bow-shot."

of a quarter of a century, have been left for the amusement of posterity by two gossiping chroniclers, Walpole and Greville. The latter writes (in August 1818)—"On Sunday we amused ourselves with eating fruit in the garden, and shooting at a mark with pistols, and playing with the monkeys. I bathed in the cold bath in the Grotto, which is as clear as crystal, and as cold as ice. Oatlands is the worst-managed establishment in England: there are a great many servants, and nobody waits on you; a great number of horses, and none to ride or drive." The parties took place every Saturday, the guests leaving on Monday morning. The Duke's favourite amusement seems to have been whist; the Duchess's, petting animals, and especially dogs, of which she had always forty or fifty. When any of these died, they were buried with great care in a space specially reserved for the purpose, each being supplied with a grave-stone, and an epitaph written by the Duchess, or some courtly sympathiser.

In 1856, Oatlands was purchased by a joint-stock company, and converted into an hotel, from the designs of Wyatt. It now presents the appearance of a very handsome Italian mansion, which, being situated on an elevated ascent, overlooks the graceful reaches of the Thames from Kingston to Windsor. The great lake, Broadwater, sleeps just below the terrace. The park is rich in timber and shrubbery, but a considerable portion of its area is now occupied by first-class villas.

OLD PUMP, WALTON.

CHAPTER VI.

WEYBRIDGE TO DATCHET.

WEYBRIDGE, FROM SHEPPERTON.

THIS but a pleasant saunter to Weybridge, the picturesque village which lies just above the confluence of the Wey with the Thames. It has a sunny Green, a handsome Decorated Church, green lanes lined by blooming hedges, and fair broad meadows stretching along the undulations of the Wey. The memorial-column to the Duchess of York, conspicuous on the Green, once formed the convergence-point of the seven streets known as Seven Dials.

> "Where fam'd St. Giles's ancient limits spread,
> An inrail'd column rears its lofty head ;
> Here to seven streets seven dials count the day,
> And from each other catch the circling ray."

Opposite Weybridge Common stands the Roman Catholic Chapel of St. Charles Borromeo, formerly used as the mausoleum of Louis Philippe and his family. Louis Philippe was interred here, with three of his daughters and five of his grandchildren, but their remains were removed to France in 1876, and deposited in the Orleans sepultuary chapel at Dreux.

Weybridge Church, erected in 1848, and enlarged in 1863, is a good specimen of Early Decorated. It contains some interesting memorials which formerly belonged to the old church: namely, that to Vice-Admiral Sir Thomas Hopson, died 1717, who broke the boom at Vigo; and another to the sisters Katherine and Mary Horneck, the "Little Comedy" and "Jessamy Bride" who threw a gleam of light across the troubled life of Oliver Goldsmith. There is also a noticeable marble monument, with kneeling figure, life size, by Chantrey, of Frederica Charlotte Ulrica Katherine, Duchess of York, died 1820.

Lingering thus long on the Surrey side of the river, we have omitted to bestow a glance, though the scene well deserved it, on Shepperton Church and village, the next point of interest above Halliford. The beautiful grounds of the Manor House form such a picture as would have tempted the vivid pencil of Claude; while the neighbouring church, which stands close by the waterside, and the group of houses around it, sheltered by leafy elms, add a charm and a character to the picture such as Claude

CONFLUENCE OF THE WEY AND THAMES.

never knew. Having a great love for the worthy band of scholars to whom England owes the rise of the New Learning, we are pleased to remember that Grocyn, the eminent Grecist, and the friend and correspondent of Erasmus, officiated here as parish priest from 1504 to 1513.

Again we cross the river, which at this point is held in high esteem by the brethren of the rod, and, passing the confluence of the silver Wey, we skirt the green expanse of Chertsey Mead, and arrive at the thrice-famous market town of Chertsey (Cerota's ey, or island). Thrice-famous—for, first, it was once the site of a splendid abbey; second, it sheltered Cowley the poet in his latter days; and third, it is close to St. Anne's Hill, the favourite and favoured residence of the statesman, Charles James Fox.

The town stands among pleasant, furzy meads, a short distance from the bank of the river—which is spanned by a neat stone bridge of seven arches, built by James Pain—and it has a station on the South-Western Railway. To the north-west rise the foliaged sides of St. Anne's Hill; southward stretches an open and agreeable country. The town itself is decorous and quiet; consisting chiefly of two long streets, crossing each other in the centre, and named London, Guildford, and Windsor Streets, according to the direction in which they point. The church stands near the heart of the town, and close to the Town Hall. A market is held every Wednesday. Little more have we to say of Chertsey, except that carrots were first cultivated here in England.

On the north side of Guildford Street we remark Cowley House, where the poet took up his residence in April, 1665, hoping to realise his old dream of "a little convenient estate, a little cheerful home, a little company, and a very little feast," and to consecrate what remained to him of life "to those studies to which Nature had so motherly inclined him," but "from which Fortune, like a stepmother, had so long detained him." The vanity of human wishes, however, was very strikingly illustrated by Cowley's rural experiences. The Arcadian solitudes he desired were no more to be found than the Arcadian innocence. "I thought," he confesses, "when I went first to dwell in the country, that without doubt I should have met there with the simplicity of the old poetical Golden Age. I thought to have found no inhabitants there but such as the shepherds of Sir Philip Sidney in Arcadia, or of Mons. d'Urfé upon the banks of Lignon; and

CHERTSEY.

began to consider with myself which way I might recommend no less to posterity the happiness and innocence of the men of Chertsey: but, to confess the truth, I perceived quickly by infallible demonstration that I was still in Old England, and not in Arcadia or La Forrest." He was equally unsuccessful as regards health. "The first night that I came hither," he writes, "I caught so great a cold, with a defluxion of rheum, as made me keep my chamber ten days; and, two after, had such a bruise on my ribs with a fall, that I am yet unable to turn myself in my bed. This is my personal fortune here to begin with. And, besides, I can get no money from my tenants, and have my meadows eaten up every night by cattle put in by my neighbours." His biographer, Bishop Sprat, tells us that, having languished under his cold for some months, he seemed to be delivered from its worst symptoms. "But in the heat of the last summer, by staying too long amongst his labourers in the meadows, he was taken with a violent defluxion, and stoppage in his breast or throat. This he at first neglected as an ordinary cold, and refused to send for his usual physicians, till it was past all remedies; and so in the end, after a fortnight's sickness, it proved mortal to him." Spence, however, ascribes his death to a different cause. "It was occasioned," he says, "by a mere accident, whilst his great friend, Dean Sprat, was with him on a visit. They had been together to see a neighbour of Cowley's, who (according to the fashion of these times) made them too welcome, They did not set out for their walk home till it was too late; and had drunk so deep, that they lay out in the fields all night. This gave Cowley the fever that carried him off" (July 21, 1607). The story reminds us of the scandalous gossip which professes to account for Shakespeare's death.

In Chertsey Church an oval marble tablet commemorates "the best of husbands, and the most excellent of men," Charles James Fox. The house where he spent some of his happiest hours, St. Anne's, is situated on the south-east side of St. Anne's Hill; an ascent of 240 feet, which, like Richmond Hill and St. George's Hill, seems intended by nature as a belvedere, or prospect-tower, from which the delighted eye may range over a vast extent of various landscape. St. Anne's contains some memorials of the great orator, large-minded statesman, and genial friend, whose name will ever be associated with it. Here Fox was seen at his best. Here he enjoyed, with keenest relish, the sweet sights and sounds of nature. Here he luxuriated in the delights of a bland day in June, or of a fragrant April morning, with "a sweet westerly wind, a beautiful sun, all the thorns and elms just budding, and the nightingales just beginning to sing." In one of his letters he remarks:—"If ever there was a place that might be called the seat of true happiness, St. Anne's is that place." It is pleasant to think of him as, walking slowly, and with gouty feet, along his garden-alleys, he expanded his ample breast to draw in the breath of the fresh breeze, and from time to time exclaimed, "Oh, how fine a thing is life!" "Oh, how glorious a thing is summer weather!"

A few words must be said as to Chertsey Abbey. It was the first religious house founded in Surrey, and its first abbot was Erconwald, afterwards Bishop of London (675). From the old English Kings it received many grants of lands and privileges; but about 894 it was destroyed by the Danes, who slaughtered its abbot and its ninety monks. Re-established by Edgar, in 964, it waxed exceedingly prosperous, its head being recognised as a mitred abbot, and a baron by tenure. When dissolved by Henry VIII., its annual income was estimated at £660. Its buildings once covered an area of four acres, but scarcely any remains have survived the hand of the spoiler. The only certain vestiges are the arched gateway and adjoining wall of a large barn, across the Abbey Bourne or River. But from excavations made on the site (now covered by a market-garden), it is known that the Abbey Church measured 275 feet in length by 63 feet in width. Among the souvenirs which earth has yielded to the explorer may be mentioned some admirable encaustic pavement tiles, richly carved capitals of Purbeck marble, a metal chalice and paten, and a coffin, also of Purbeck marble. The Abbey fish-ponds, or "stews," are still extant.

Passing through Chertsey Lock (observe here the brightness of the landscape, including, as it does, the green summit of St. Anne's and the wooded rise of Woburn), we come to

Laleham, on the Middlesex side. It is one of the quietest of the river-villages, and its scenery is unquestionably tame. Yet to the present writer it has a special attraction, from its connection with a man who may justly be spoken of as both great and good, the late Dr. Arnold, who, as Head Master of Rugby, exercised so beneficial an influence upon our public school system. Arnold lived here from 1819 until his removal to Rugby in 1828. "Years after he had left it," says Dr. Stanley, "he still retained his early affection for it, and, till he had purchased his house in Westmoreland, he entertained a lingering hope that he might return to it in his old age, when he should have retired from Rugby. Often he would revisit it, and delighted in renewing his acquaintance with all the families of the poor whom he had known during his residence; in showing to his children his former haunts; in looking once again on his favourite views of the great plain of Middlesex—the lovely walks along the quiet banks of the Thames—the retired garden, with its 'Campus Martius,' and its 'wilderness of trees,' which lay behind his house, and which had been the scenes of so many sportive games and serious conversations—the churchyard of Laleham, now doubly dear to him, as containing the graves of his infant child, whom he buried there in 1832, and of his mother, his aunt, and his sister." Dr. Arnold's house and the Earl of Lucan's mansion are the only two points of interest in the village.

PONTON HOOK.

Ponton Hook, or "Ponty Hook," is a spot well known to anglers. Barbel and chub are literally plentiful in its neighbourhood. An artificial "cut" shortens the navigation of the river by about a mile, and helps us onward to Staines Bridge, a handsome structure of stone, designed by Rennie, and erected in 1832. Here the Colne flows into the Thames. Staines is generally identified with the Roman *Pontes*, whence started the great Roman road across Surrey to Silchester. It is called "Stanes" in Domesday Book, a fact which seems to get rid of the theory that it owes its modern name to the boundary stone (now in a meadow near the bridge) marking the western limit of the jurisdiction of the City of London over the Thames. A quieter, cleaner, or more dully respectable town than Staines it would be difficult to find; yet it boasts of some considerable manufactories, and in the summer season brightens up with a crowd of visitors, attracted by its facilities for boating and fishing. Staines Deep is a favourite haunt of roach. "Deeps," by the way, are those portions of the Thames which have been protected by stakes and other appliances from the encroachment of nets.

On the Surrey side of the river, but a short distance inland, lies the well-to-do and well-looking village of Egham; a convenient centre from which to visit Virginia Water (three miles), Windsor Great Park (two miles), and Cooper's Hill (about one mile). Its church contains the wonderfully hideous and colossal monument, crowded with skeletons and effigies, of Sir John Denham, Chief Baron of the Exchequer, and father of the poet (died 1638). His seat, of old called the Place, is now the Vicarage, but it retains its

VIEW FROM COOPER'S HILL.

Jacobean character, and is still, as it was in old Aubrey's time, "a house very convenient, not great, but pretty, and healthily situated."

Cooper's Hill, a long ridge of the Bagshot Sand, stretching to the north-west, is famous for those fine prospects which Sir John Denham has described in such vigorous verse. Of the Hill itself he speaks with poetic extravagance:—

> "But his proud head the airy mountain hides
> Among the clouds; his shoulders and his sides
> A shady mountain clothes; his crested brows
> Frown on the gentle stream, which calmly flows,
> While winds and storms his lofty forehead beat—
> The common fate of all that's high or great."

His felicitous description of the Thames is well known:—

> "Thames, the most lov'd of all the ocean's sons
> By his old sire, to his embraces runs,
> Hasting to pay his tribute to the sea,
> Like mortal life to meet eternity. . . .
> O, could I flow like thee, and make thy stream
> My great example, as it is my theme!
> Though deep, yet clear; though gentle, yet not dull;
> Strong without rage, without o'erflowing full."

Denham's poem was first published in 1643, and at once took up that respectable position among our English classics which it still enjoys. Dryden praised it as "the exact standard of good writing;" Dr. Johnson characterised its author as the founder* of "a species of composition that may be denominated local poetry, of which the fundamental subject is some particular landscape to be locally described, with the addition of such embellishments as may be supplied by historical retrospection or incidental meditation;" and Pope gracefully exclaims:—

> "On Cooper's Hill eternal wreaths shall grow,
> While lasts the mountain, or while Thames shall flow."

The view from the crest of Cooper's Hill assuredly deserves poetical celebration. It is more extensive, and, to our thinking, more varied and effective than that from St. Anne's, or even from Richmond Hill. The landscape derives a special lustre from the windings of the ample river—its bosom studded with osier-green eyots, and its banks lined with green meadows, or blooming gardens, or leafy groves—and a certain dignity from the stately towers of royal Windsor, which rise majestically above dense masses of foliage, and trace the noble avenue known as the Long Walk.

On the west side of the Hill stands the splendid pile of the Indian Civil Engineering College, over which Colonel George Chesney presides.

At its base spreads the long verdurous level of Runnimede, historically celebrated as the scene where King John attached his reluctant signature to the Great Charter (June, 1215). Says Sir John Denham:—

> "Low at his foot a spacious plain is plac'd,
> Between the mountain and the stream embrac'd,
> Which shade and shelter from the hill derives,
> While the kind river wealth and beauty gives; . . .
> Here was that Charter seal'd wherein the Crown
> All marks of arbitrary power lays down."

Akenside wrote an inscription for a memorial column which it was purposed to raise here. It was never erected, however, and the Egham Races are its substitute!

Various etymologies of the word "Runnimede" have been put forward; but the most probable traces it to the Old-English *rune* (council), because here, in ancient times, "the councils concerning the safety of the Commonwealth" *(ibi de pace regni sæpius consilia)* assembled. The mead is about 160 acres in extent, and fenced from the Thames by a raised causeway, constructed in the reign of Henry III. It is bounded by Longmead on the west, and Yardmead on the south-east.

Nearer the opposite bank, and a little higher up the river, lies Charter Island (two and a-half acres), included in the parish of Wraysbury, or Wyrardisbury, Buckinghamshire. It was the scene, in September, 1217, of the treaty between Prince Henry (afterwards Henry III.) and the confederate Barons, by which their ally, Prince Louis of

---

* The critic must have forgotten Ben Jonson's poem on "Penshurst."

France, agreed to quit the country. Its modern name perpetuates an erroneous tradition, for the Great Charter was not signed on the island, but on the meadow.

Before we take leave of this locality, we must make reference to Englefield Green, a high and open tract of verdure about one mile westward of Egham, with quite a colony of "seats" and "mansions," of which Round Oak, belonging to the Marquis of Carmarthen, may be considered the head. The "Green" should be visited in memory of the beautiful and frail actress, Mrs. Robinson, the unhappy "Perdita" of George IV.'s pretended love-romance. She resided for some years in Englefield Green Cottage, and died there, at the early age of 43, on the 26th of December, 1800. It is curious to read of the princely "Florizel's" commonplace devices—thus: "After we had corresponded," she says, "some months without ever speaking to each other (for I still declined meeting his Royal Highness, from a dread of the *éclat* which such a connexion would produce, and the fear of injuring him in the opinion of his Royal relatives), I received, through the hands of Lord Maldon, the Prince's portrait in miniature, painted by the late Mr. Myers. . . . Within the case was a small heart cut in paper. . . . On one side was written, '*Je ne change qu'en mordant.*' On the other, 'Unalterable to my Perdita through life.'"

At the age of twenty-four, Mrs. Robinson became an incurable cripple; and a striking moral may be drawn from the following account of one of her later appearances in London society. "At a table, in a waiting-room of the Opera House, was seated a woman of fashionable appearance, still beautiful, but not in the bloom of beauty's pride; she was not noticed, except by the eye of pity. In a few minutes two liveried servants came to her, and they took from their pockets long white sleeves, which they drew on their arms; they then lifted her up and conveyed her to her carriage; it was the then helpless, paralytic Perdita!"

SHEPPERTON.

LAKE AT VIRGINIA WATER

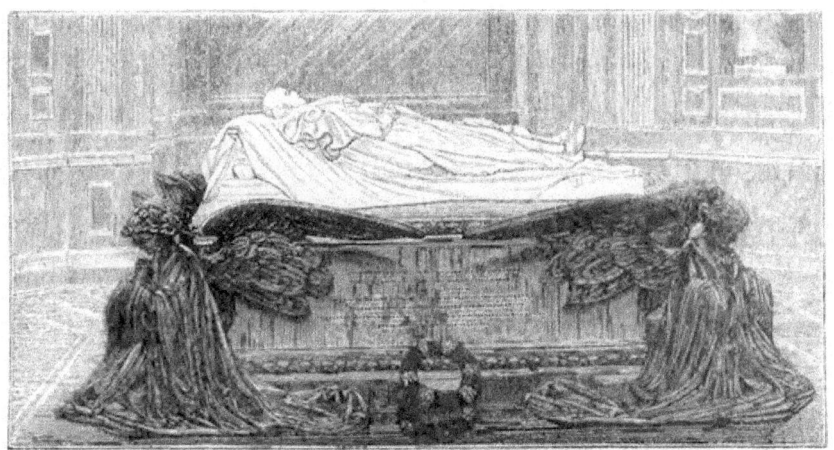

PRINCE CONSORT'S TOMB.

CHAPTER VII.

HORTON—OLD WINDSOR—DATCHET—WINDSOR—THE GREAT PARK—FROGMORE.

OME short distance inland, on the Middlesex side of the river, lies one of the most honoured shrines of English Pilgrimage; Horton, the residence, for nearly six years, of John Milton. Here, after leaving Cambridge, he devoted himself to the study of the Greek and Latin writers; in the intervals of this grave pursuit composing some of his most exquisite sonnets, his "Lycidas," "Comus," the "Arcades," and the two companion pictures of "L'Allegro" and "Il Penseroso." Of these the colouring was evidently derived from the sweet pastoral scenery around Horton. It was there that, every day, he saw—

" Meadows trim with daisies pied,
Shallow brooks and rivers wide '—

the Colne and the Thames; and there, too, that he looked across to Windsor's royal pile, with its towers and battlements

" Bosomed high in tufted trees."

In this neighbourhood, as the year revolved, his eye must often have rested on

"Russet lawns and fallows grey,
Where the nibbling flocks 'did' stray;"

and, in his early walks, he could not fail to hear the far sounds of the ringing music, when

> " Hounds and horn
> Cheerily roused the slumbering morn,
> From the side of some hoar hill,
> Through the high wood echoing shrill."

The following passage has a sweet savour of pleasant Horton about it:—

> "Some time walking, not unseen,
> By hedge-row elms, on hillocks green,
> Right against the eastern gate,
> Where the great sun begins his state,
> Robed in flames and amber light,
> The clouds in thousand liveries dight;
> While the ploughman, near at hand,
> Whistles o'er the furrow'd land;
> And the milkmaid singeth blithe.
> And the mower whets his scythe.'

The poet's house, unfortunately, has been swept away; its site is now occupied by Byrken Manor House. His mother, Sara, lies interred in the ancient, ivy-shrouded, square-towered church.

On the Berkshire bank of the river—for we have passed the bounds of " sunny Surrey "—Old Windsor now claims our attention. The parent of the neighbouring and more prosperous "royal burgh" of New Windsor, it derives its name (anciently Windlesora) from the sinuous course which the beautiful river at this point adopts. In very early times it was a royal "vill;" and here Edward the Confessor sometimes dwelt in kingly state. On one of these occasions flamed out the fierce quarrel between Harold and his impetuous brother, Tostig, which exercised so evil an influence on the fate of the " Last of the English Kings." William the Conqueror was partial to Windlesora, from its vicinity to the great forest where he was wont to indulge his passion for the chase; but he had no liking for the comparatively low situation of the English palace, and built for himself a royal castle on the ascent now covered by Windsor's magnificent pile. The site of the ancient palace was indicated until recently by a farm, which, surrounded by a moat, stood near the river, to the west of the church. The moat may still be traced.

VICTORIA BRIDGE.

Old Windsor Church, a building of the thirteenth century, was restored by Sir G. G.

Scott, in 1864. In the graveyard is buried Mrs. Mary Robinson, the celebrated actress, who, as "Perdita," in "The Winter's Tale," charmed the fancy of the Prince of Wales (George IV.), and afterwards became his mistress. There was an air of mock romance thrown over the connection, and the Prince delighted to pose as "Florizel;" but the end of it, as we have already seen, was sad enough to propitiate the severest moralist. To the south of the village, on a conspicuous eminence, stands the Roman Catholic College of St. Stanislaus; formerly, as Beaumont, the seat of our great Indian proconsul, Warren Hastings.

Re-crossing the river, we arrive at the delectable village of Datchet, connected with Windsor by the graceful span of Mr. Page's Victoria Bridge (there is an Albert Bridge lower down, opposite Old Windsor), beyond which are visible the deep leafy masses of the Home Park, and the pretty island known by the unpoetic name of Black Pots. The Great Western Railway crosses the river just above; and a remarkably picturesque "bit" for the sketcher's note-book is afforded by Windsor Lock. The low ground stretching between the river and Windsor Little Park is Datchet Mead, where Falstaff met with signal

DATCHET.

punishment at the hands of the "Merry Wives," and was well soused in the cooling waters of the Thames. "Being thus crammed in the basket," he tells Master Brook, "a couple of Ford's knaves, his hinds, were called forth by their mistress, to carry me in the name of foul clothes to Datchet Lane; they took me on their shoulders; met the jealous knave their master in the door, who asked them once or twice what they had in their basket: I quaked for fear, lest the lunatic knave would have searched it; but fate, ordaining he should be a cuckold, held his hand. Well: on he went for a search, and away went I for foul clothes. But mark the sequel, Master Brook. I suffered the pangs of three several deaths: first, an intolerable fright, to be detected with a jealous, rotten bell-wether; next, to be compassed, like a good bilbo, in the circumference of a peck, hilt to point, heel to head; and then, to be stopped in, like a strong distillation, with stinking clothes, that fretted in their own grease. . . . And in the height of this bath, when I was more than half-stewed in grease, like a Dutch dish, to be thrown into the Thames, and cooled, glowing hot, in that surge, like a horse-shoe: think of that—hissing hot—think of that, Master Brook."

FROM DATCHET TO ETON.

The Mead lies on the Windsor, and not, as its name would suggest, on the Datchet side of the river. As Shakespeare describes it, the shore here is "shelvy and shallow."

Datchet is not interesting in itself, but in its surroundings. Lovelier scenery of its kind, and to us it is a very lovely kind—you will hardly discover within the three seas; nor scenery more characteristically English—that is, green with a perennial greenness, soft in outline, vivid yet harmonious in colouring, steeped in calm, and yet not without an air of majesty. This it owes to the grand feature of the Castle, which, with its great Tower, when lit up by the hues of sunset, acquires a luminous splendour and a degree of aerial pomp indescribable by words. Woods and sloping lawns, broad stretches of meadow and delicate bits of garden bloom, are diversified by the architectural forms of goodly mansions or picturesque cottages; while the flashing river, with its changeful tints and fairy-like reflections, is a constant source of beauty and delight.

The river, from Datchet up to Eton, has always been a favourite resort of anglers. Here came their prince and patriarch, Izaak Walton, fishing for a "little trout, called a samlet or skagger trout, that would bite as fast and freely as minnows." Here his disciple, Charles Cotton, fished with him, enjoying his varied and weighty discourse; and Dr. Donne, the most crabbed of poets; and Sir Henry Wotton, who, after a stirring diplomatic career, passed into lettered and leisured retirement as Provost of Eton. Wotton, who found angling, after tedious study, "a cheerer of his spirits, a diverter of sadness, a calmer of unquiet thoughts, a moderator of passions, a procurer of contentedness," built for himself a fishing-lodge on the site now occupied by the cottage called Black Pots. It was there that, one summer evening, as he sat on a bank "a-fishing," he wrote the beautiful lines descriptive of Spring which Walton has preserved:—

"This day Dame Nature seemed in love;
The lusty sap began to move;
Fresh juice did stir th' embracing vines,
And birds have drawn their valentines.
The jealous trout, that low did lie,
Rose at a well-dissembled fly;
There stood my friend, with patient skill,
Attending on his trembling quill.
Already were the eaves possest
With the swift pilgrim's daubèd nest;
The groves already did rejoice

In Philomel's triumphant voice;
The showers were sport, the weather mild,
The morning fresh, the evening smiled.
Joan takes her neat-rubbed pail, and now
She trips to milk the sand-red cow,
Where, for some sturdy foot-ball swain,
Joan strokes a syllabub or twain.
The fields and gardens were beset
With tulips, crocus, violet;
And now, though late, the modest rose
Did more than half a blush disclose."

Verrio, the painter, erected a summer villa on the site of Wotton's fishing-house. Charles II. frequently resorted to this part of the river to trifle away an hour or two with rod and line. "But see," exclaims Rochester, satirically,—

"But see, he now does up from Datchet come,
Laden with spoils of slaughtered gudgeons home."

At length we reach Windsor, "the most famous place within the environs of London," and, in some respects, the most famous in this island; one which is known and honoured wherever English-speaking men and women dwell.

Of the "royal burgh," however, little need be said, and there is little to say. Were it not for the mighty pile that overshadows it, it would rank among the more commonplace English towns; for it possesses no important remains of antiquity, no conspicuous public building, no memorials of English worthies. It has no history, or what it has is virtually absorbed in that of the Castle. It consists of a main street, curving from the Castle gate to the extremity of the Eton bridge, of another principal thoroughfare, Peascod Street, and of some smaller highways and byeways. Its Town Hall was originally built by Sir Christopher Wren, to whom also are attributed the Bank and the Free School. All its churches are modern, but it has a few antique houses, one of which, the Duke's Head Inn,

BLACK POTS

is traditionally reputed to have been the residence of Villiers, Duke of Buckingham. The Garter Inn, immortalised by Shakespeare, has ceased to exist; and the houses of the "Merry Wives" know their places no more.

Windsor lives by and for the Castle; and the visitor's first impulse, when once he has set foot within its precincts, is to bend his steps to the Home of England's Kings. Like many first impulses, this, we think, is a mistake. Let him first view the Castle from the river, from Datchet, from the Great Park, and allow its stately proportions to sink into his mind. That is, let him submit himself to the influence of the *genius loci*. Then he may proceed to examine it in detail. Some of the glimpses which may be snatched from vantage-points in the surrounding country, and especially from the Great Park, where it closes up in the grandest imaginable manner each splendid vista, stir the imagination powerfully. In no other way is it possible fully to realise the nobleness of this royal pile, and its fitness to be the chief palace and residence of the sovereign of the British Empire.

There is nothing more beautiful of its kind in the United Kingdom than the Great Park. Valleys, and green paths, and "bowery hollows;" breadths of velvety sward; clumps of patriarchal trees, standing "knee-deep in fern," and warped by the winds of many winters into strange, picturesque shapes; hushed woodland solitudes, which the fancy hastens to people with the graceful creations of the older creed,

"While visions, as poetic eyes avow,
Cling to each leaf, and swarm on every bough;"

long shadowy avenues of elm, and beech, and chestnut; for days the explorer may wander at

WINDSOR CASTLE FROM THE RIVER.

his will, and ever find something new to admire. It was this haunted woodland which suggested to Shelley the sylvan scenery of his "Alastor." The poet dreamed away the days, we are told, in the oaken shades of Windsor Great Park; and its various aspects were well fitted to inspire the conception of the vivid forest landscapes that enrich and embellish the poem. Such as the following :—

" The meeting boughs, and implicated leaves,
    Wove twilight o'er the poet's path . . .
           More dark
And dark the shades accumulate. The oak,
Expanding its immense and knotty arms,
Embraces the light beech. The pyramids
Of the tall cedar, overarching, frame
Most solemn domes within; and far below,
Like clouds suspended in an emerald sky,
The ash and the acacia floating hang,
Tremulous and pale."

To not a few of our landscape artists the forest has supplied rich and rare material.

THE LODGES—THE HOME PARK.

The area covered by the Great Park, if we include the Crown enclosures of the old Windsor Forest, must consist of about 3800 acres. Throughout its entire length it is traversed by the Long Walk (three miles), begun by Charles II. and completed by William III. This noble avenue, with its double border of venerable elms, extends from the Castle Gate to Sand Hill, an eminence crowned by Westmacott's colossal equestrian statue of George III. Another and longer avenue, lined by a single row of elms, reaches from Hudson's Gate to the southern limit of the Park. It owes its existence to "good Queen Anne," and is still known as Queen Anne's Ride.

There are three lodges—the Royal, Cumberland, and Cranborne. The Royal Lodge was built by George IV., who spent the closing years of his reign in this retreat, anxiously avoiding the slightest publicity, and wholly ignorant that his Clerk of the Council (as we shall hereafter see) was preparing to lift the curtain from the royal retirement, with

WINDSOR CASTLE FROM THE LONG WALK.

unscrupulous boldness, for the amusement of posterity. Cumberland Lodge was seriously damaged by fire in 1869, but was rebuilt and refitted for the residence of the Prince and Princess Christian. It was erected by Charles II., but owes its name to William Duke of Cumberland (the "Culloden" Duke), who occupied it during his rangership of the Park. Cranborne Lodge, situated on a gentle rise, and commanding some fair prospects, is used as a resting-place for the royal party during their longer walks and drives from the Castle.

About seventeen hundred deer are kept in the Park; and their appearance frequently contributes to the picturesqueness of the landscape. There is also a heronry near Sandpit Gate.

The Home Park, over which Shakespeare has thrown the rich light of his glorious humour in the "Merry Wives of Windsor," has an area of about 500 acres, and lies to the north and east of the Castle—that is, between the Castle and the Thames. It is no longer open to the public. Though deficient in variety of surface, it gains a beauty of its own from the number and stateliness of its trees, which are here grouped in grand masses, there set forth in long imposing avenues, or scattered about singly, with sweeping branches that create delightful oases of shade. Of old it could boast of the tree of trees, Shakespeare's tree—that "Herne's Oak" round which the hunter,

"Sometime a keeper here in Windsor Forest."

was doomed to walk "all the winter time;" beneath whose boughs the pretended fairies did so "pinch," and "burn," and "turn about" Falstaff, that "man of middle earth." Herne's Oak, with its "great rugged horns," was cut down by mistake in the spring of 1796. Many persons, it should be stated, contend that the veritable oak was a tall and withered tree, near the elm avenue, which fell on the 31st of August, 1863, the site of which is now marked by a young oak;* but there can be little doubt of the inaccuracy of their belief. In the neighbourhood of Cranborne Lodge flourishes a huge oak, known as "William the Conqueror's;" while "within a clearing in the wood, on the other side of the Winkfield road, thrives a splendid oak, the trunk rising straight and clear for some 80 feet before the branches spread out into a stately head," which bears the name of "Queen Victoria's Tree."

END OF THE LONG WALK.

Frogmore House, which was successively the residence of Queen Charlotte, the Princess Augusta, and the Duchess of Kent, now belongs to Her Majesty. Here are the Royal Garden (about 30 acres), prodigal of fruit and flowers, and the exquisite bijou of the Royal Dairy. Here, too, on the artificial mound which rises near the ornamental water, stands the Mausoleum of the Duchess of Kent, erected from the designs of Mr. Humbert in 1873. It forms a circular temple of Portland stone, surrounded by sixteen Ionic columns, their bases and capitals of bronze, their shafts of gleaming grey granite, highly polished. The cupola is of copper; of bronze, the doorway with the door. The granite sarcophagus which encloses the Duchess's remains occupies the lower or ground chamber; in an upper one is her statue, by Theed.

The elaborate and costly Mausoleum of the Prince Consort, on which was spent the labour and love of nine years (1862 to 1870), is situated in this direction. It is visible from

---

* Planted by the Queen on the 12th of September following.

CASCADE AT VIRGINIA WATER

the Castle. Its ground plan is that of a cross with limbs of equal length, the interspaces being filled with small chapels. The octagonal lantern, which forms the centre, is surmounted by a cross. At the east end is placed the entrance porch. Dimensions of the whole :—80 feet by 70 feet, and 83 feet high to the top of the lantern. The walls are of beautifully polished stone, relieved by columns of polished granite. The general effect is rich and dignified, without heaviness; and the architect, Mr. Humbert, may be considered to have succeeded in an unquestionably difficult task. Internally, Professor Grüner's decorations, in the Cinque-Cento style, are marked by their costliness and abundance. Not a foot of space has been left vacant ; the eye is almost wearied by the *embarras de richesses*. The walls glow with coloured marbles, contrasting with the pure white marble shafts of the columns, and harmonising with their gilded capitals, bases, and mouldings. There are also arabesques, pictures, mosaics, gilded angels, frescoes of the Evangelists, statues of the Prophets, decorated work in gilt bronze ; all fused together, however, with a splendid unity and true artistic feeling. The sarcophagus, which rests upon a base of black marble, was hewn out of the largest block of Aberdeen granite ever quarried. The recumbent effigy of the Prince Consort, in white marble, which ornaments the lid, was executed by the late Baron Marochetti. *(See cut, p. 49.)*

MAUSOLEUM.

CHAPTER VIII.

WINDSOR CASTLE: ITS HISTORY.

> "To that supremest place of the great English Kings,
> The Garter's royal seat, from him who did advance
> That princely Order first, and first that vanquished France ;
> The temple of St. George, whereat his honour'd Knights,
> Upon his hallowed day, observe their ancient rites :
> Where Eton is at hand to nurse that learned brood,
> To keep the Muses still near to this princely flood,
> That nothing there may want to beautify that seat,
> With every pleasure stored. . . . . . .
> MICHAEL DRAYTON, *Poly-Olbion*, Song xv.

WINDSOR CASTLE might not inaptly be termed the history of England in stone. It forms a kind of national chronicle, recording the names of our Kings, and suggesting many of the great events in which they figured. For upwards of seven centuries it has been the residence of the Sovereign ; the scene of courtly gatherings, of regal shows, of national councils. It may be held, not altogether fancifully, to typify our English character—and that Constitution which bears its impress—in its happy conservation of antiquity, and its adaptation to modern wants and uses. The work of William the Norman and the work of Victoria blend together without any sense of incongruity. However this may be, no one will deny that its appearance is singularly impressive, that it looks the fit home of mighty Kings. "It is in truth," says a sympathetic writer, "a palace worthy of our Monarchs, rising proudly on a steep which commands prospects unrivalled on all sides." Says Mr. Thorne :—" Seated on an eminence which overlooks the broad valley of the Thames, with the town at its base, the massive proportions of the Castle—its proud keep, and long array of turrets, walls, and battlements—display themselves to great advantage, whilst from towers, windows, and terraces stretches far away 'that incomparable prospect,' as it was designated two centuries ago, which fills every one with wonder and delight when gazed upon for the first time, and which no familiarity renders wearisome."

A castle seems to have been planted on this height before the Conquest. William enlarged and strengthened it, confiding the charge of it to William Fitz-Other, first

"Constable of Windsor Castle." It was inhabited by William Rufus, who at one time imprisoned here the Earl of Northumberland and his partisans on a charge of treason.

In 1106, Henry I. held his court at Windsor, and received not only his English barons,

OLD WINDSOR LOCK.

but those of Normandy. Here, in 1122, he married Adeleis, or Alice of Louvain; and here, four years later, assembled the Great Council which nominated his daughter, the Empress Matilda, as his successor. The first to take the oath of fealty was David, King of Scotland. He was followed by Stephen, Earl of Boulogne, and then by the English Barons in order of precedence, each one pledging himself to maintain his succession.

Stephen and Henry II., in due course, dwelt beneath its roof; and the latter, in his unhappy old age, when his sons had rebelled against him, caused to be painted on the walls of his chamber the grimmest of allegories—an old eagle, with three eaglets pecking at its body and a fourth at its eyes—the eagle representing himself, the three eaglets his sons, Henry, Richard, and Geoffry, and the fourth, the youngest and basest, John. John spent some troubled months at Windsor.*

The Castle was twice besieged by the Barons in the time of Henry III. (1217 and 1263), to whom it owed additions of such importance, that Matthew of Westminster declared it to be the stateliest royal residence in Europe. He built a new and superb chapel, a grand hall, and various royal apartments. But such was his lack of funds that, on one occasion, to pay his workmen, he was compelled to pawn "the best image of the Virgin Mary" which had been set up in the new Chapel Royal. Splendid tournays were held within its precincts by Edward I.; and Edward II. made it his principal abode. By the third Edward, who was born here, it was almost entirely rebuilt, and on a scale of splendour worthy of the most splendid of the Plantagenets, as well as of the genius of his architect, William of Wykeham, Bishop of Winchester. We read that "three hundred and sixty workmen were required to be employed on the building at the King's wages: some of whom having clandestinely left Windsor, and engaged on other employments to greater advantage, writs were issued prohibiting all persons from employing them, on pain of forfeiting all their goods and chattels." Edward built the Round Tower, the Rose Tower, the Upper Ward, cloisters and arcades, a treasury, chapter-house, deanery, halls and towers, and other edifices; and he almost entirely rebuilt the chapel founded by Henry III. Besides William of Wykeham (1356-1362), John Peynton, Richard de Rotheley, Robert de Burnham, and William de Mulso were employed as surveyors or clerks of the works; but all appear to have been guided by some definite principles of construction. The Round Tower we may suppose to have been Edward's own "idea." It was erected in 1343, with all possible rapidity, in order that the chivalrous monarch might hold within its walls his great "international" tournament of the Round Table, in honour of King Arthur. This gorgeous spectacle began on the 19th of January, 1344, when the famous Order of the Garter was instituted.

The romantic tradition† that this Order originated in a mishap which befell the beautiful Countess of Salisbury while she was dancing with King Edward, is contradicted by the fact that Richard Cœur-de-Lion had previously founded a brotherhood of Knights of the Blue Garter. That she was considered, however, to be concerned in its revival, would appear to be evident from Froissart's words:—"You have all heard," he says,

---

* He went from Windsor to sign the Great Charter at Runnimede; and returned to the Castle after that memorable scene.

† "The popular account is, that during a festival at court, a lady happened to drop her garter, which was taken up by King Edward, who, observing a significant smile among the bystanders, exclaimed with some displeasure, 'Honi soit qui mal y pense'—'Shame to him who thinks ill of it.' In the spirit of gallantry, which belonged no less to the age than to his own disposition, conformably with the custom of wearing a lady's favour, and perhaps to prevent any further impertinence, the King is said to have placed the garter round his own knee."—TIGHE AND DAVIS, *Annals of Windsor*.

"how passionately King Edward was smitten with the charms of that noble lady. Out of affection to her, and his desire to see her, he proclaimed a great feast in August, 1343. He commanded all his lords and knights to attend without fail, and expressly ordered the Earl of Salisbury to bring his lady the Countess, with as many young ladies as she could bring in her train. The Earl very cheerfully complied with the King's request, for he thought no evil, and his good dame durst not refuse. She came, however, much against her will, for she guessed the reason which made the King so earnest for her attendance, but was afraid to discover it to her husband, intending by her conduct and conversation to make the King change his opinion." The first chapter of the Order seems to have been held on St. George's day, 1343, when it was attended by Queen Philippa and the ladies whom Edward's chivalry associated with his knights. It is not until 1351 that we read of the members of the Order as being all attired in mantles of blue cloth, powdered over with garters, and wearing the emblematic collar. In 1358, the festival was unusually magnificent. Three royal captives were present: John, king of France, and his son, Philip, taken prisoners at Poitiers; and David of Scotland, taken prisoner at the battle of Neville's Cross. At the banquet, Edward sat between the two foreign princes, who afterwards tilted at the lists. Tradition relates that the three kings, in one of the pauses of the prolonged revel, were walking on the higher part of the castle-ridge, when the royal captives, struck by the beauty of the position, remarked that it would have been a better site for the castle than that which it then occupied, "as it would be more open to see and be seen afar off." Edward agreed, and added, that so it should be, and he would bring his castle thither; that is to say, he would extend it that distance with two other wards, "the charges whereof should be borne with their ransoms." As a matter of fact, however—and fact is a great enemy of tradition—the works were begun many years before any such conversation could have taken place.

The Black Prince and Joan, the Fair Maid of Kent, were married at Windsor on the 10th of October, 1361. The festivities ordered on this occasion fully justify the character which the poet and historian, Daniel, gives to King Edward :—" He showed his magnificence in his triumphs and feasts, which were sumptuous, with all due rites and ceremonies to preserve reverence and majesty." The wedding was graced by the presence of Queen Philippa, who, eight years later, drew her last breath in the castle that had sheltered so many of her brightest days. Froissart's account of her end is full of simple pathos :—*

"While her son, the Duke of Lancaster, was encamped in the valley of Tourneham ready to give battle to the Duke of Burgundy, this death happened in England, to the infinite misfortune of King Edward, his children, and the whole kingdom. That excellent lady the queen, who had done so much good, aiding all knights, ladies, and

---

* Froissart was Secretary to Queen Philippa from 1361 to 1366.

damsels, when distressed, who had applied to her, was at this time dangerously sick at Windsor Castle, and every day her disorder increased. When the good queen perceived that her end approached, she called to the king, and extending her right hand from under the bed-clothes, put it into the right hand of King Edward, who was oppressed with sorrow, and thus spoke:—'We have, my husband, enjoyed our long union in happiness, peace, and prosperity. But I entreat, before I depart, and we are forever separated in this world, that you will grant me three requests.' King Edward, with sighs and tears, replied, 'Lady, name them: whatever be your requests, they shall be granted.' 'My lord,' she said, 'I beg you will fulfil whatever engagements I have entered into with merchants for their wares, as well on this, as on the other side of the sea; I beseech you to fulfil whatever gifts or legacies I have made or left to churches wherein I have paid my devotions, and to all my servants, whether male or female; and when it shall please God to call you hence, you will choose no other sepulchre than mine, and that you will rest by my side in the cloisters of Westminster Abbey.' The King, in tears, replied, 'Lady, all this shall be done.' Soon after, the good lady made the sign of the cross on her breast, and having recommended to the king her youngest son, Thomas, who was present, praying to God, she gave up her spirit, which, I firmly believe, was caught by holy angels and carried to the glory of heaven, for she had never done anything by thought or deed to endanger her soul. Thus died this admirable queen of England, in the year of grace, 1369, the vigil of the Assumption of the Virgin, the 16th of August."

Passing on to the reign of Richard II., we find that he celebrated the festivals of the Garter with a sumptuousness not unworthy of his grandfather, whose taste for splendid attire he inherited. We read of his appearance in a truly royal costume, blazing with precious stones, and valued at 30,000 marks; and of his queen, Anne of Bohemia, as dressed in a robe of violet cloth, dyed in grain, and lined with fur; while the hood was lined with scarlet. At Windsor principally resided his child-wife, Isabella of Valois, married, in 1395, at the early age of eight years. It was here he parted from her in May, 1399, before he went on his first expedition: he never saw her again. The scene of their farewell was Windsor Church. He had previously attended mass, and with his melodious voice chanted a collect. After the service, he and his little queen shared together a brief repast of wine and comfits; then, taking her up in his arms, he covered her fair face with kisses, saying, "Adieu, adieu, madam, until we meet again." Let us remember also that it was here that Henry, Duke of Hereford, afterwards Henry IV., and the Duke of Norfolk, after levelling accusations of treason at each other, appealed to King Richard for leave to decide their quarrel by mortal combat. The required leave was awarded:

> " Be ready, as your lives shall answer it,
> At Coventry, upon Saint Lambert's Day.
> There shall your swords and lances arbitrate
> The swelling difference of your settled hate."

Nor must we fail to note that Geoffry Chaucer, "The Morning Star of English Poetry," acted as clerk of the works at Windsor, and supervised, from 1390 to 1393, the enlargement and embellishment of the then St. George's Chapel. The great poet,

> "Which first made to distil and rain
> The gold dew-drops of speech and eloquence
> Into English tongue,"

had just completed his "Testament of Love."

James I. of Scotland resided as a prisoner at Windsor for several years. He was only twenty when first brought thither, but it does not appear that he found his captivity a burden. He shared in all the pleasures and pastimes of the English Court, which exhibited a pomp and an affluence wholly unknown north of the Tweed. He studied the poems of Chaucer and "moral Gower;" and beguiled his leisure by making love to the Lady Joan Beaufort, daughter of the Earl of Beaufort, who afterwards became his Queen (1424). She was not less noble of heart than beautiful of person; and in all respects was worthy to have inspired "the King's Quhair" (or Book), the love-poem in which he so picturesquely celebrates her. Very sweet and natural is the royal poet's description of the circumstances under which he first saw the future mistress of his fortunes. He had risen, he says, at daybreak, to escape from the gloomy reflections of a sleepless pillow. "Bewailing in his chamber thus alone," he finds his way to the window to look out upon the freshness of the morning. This window (probably one in the Earl Marshal's Tower at the south-east corner of the Upper Ward) commanded a pleasant view of a small garden:—

> "Now was there made, fast by the Tower's wall,
> A garden fair, and in the corners set
> An arbour green, with wandis long and small
> Railèd about; and so with leaves beset
> Was all the place, and hawthorn hedges knet,
> That lyf was none* walking there forbye,
> That might within scarce any wight espy.
> So thick the boughis and the leavès green
> Beshaded all the alleys that there were,
> And midst of every arbour might be seen
> The sharpè, greenè, swetè juniper,
> Growing so fair, with branches here and there,
> That as it seemèd to a lyf without,
> The boughs did spread the arbour all about."

Suddenly the nightingale began to sing her hymn of love; and the prisoner's thoughts, attuned to the melody, wandered into a delightful dreamland. He had often read of love; what might that feeling be which poured a happy life into every vein of nature? And if it were so great a felicity, and so widely dispersed, why was he alone debarred from its enjoyment? While thus musing, he cast his eye downward, and beheld

---

* That there was no person.

"Walking under the tower
Full secretly, new comen here to plain,
The fairest and the freshest youngè flower"

he had ever seen. Immediately his heart went forth to her; it was a case of love at first sight.

He proceeds to describe the young beauty as she appeared to his enamoured vision, and sums up her perfections in some charming stanzas:—

"Of her array the form if I shall write,
Towards her golden hair and rich attire,
In fretwise couchit[a] with pearlis white
And great balas[b] gleaming as the fire,
With many an emerald and fair sapphire;
And on her head a chaplet fresh of hue,
Of plumis parted red, and white, and blue. .

"About her neck, white as the fire amail,[c]
A goodly chain of small orfevory,[d]
Whereby there hung a ruby, without fail,
Like to ane heart shapen verily,
That, as a spark of low,[e] so wantonly
Seemèd burning upon her whitè throat,
Now if there was good party,[f] God it wot.

"In her was youth, beauty, with humble aport,
Bounty, richess, and womanly feature,
God better wot than my pen can report:
Wisdom, largess, estate, and cunning sure,
In every point so guided her measùre,
In word, in deed, in shape, in countenance,
That nature might no more her child advance."

The poem is worth reading, and notwithstanding its early date, is by no means difficult reading. Some of the allegorical portions are tedious; but much of it is written with fine taste and enjoyable freshness; and its descriptions of nature are distinguished by their vividness and truth. Moreover, as a trustworthy critic says of it, as an amatory poem, it is edifying in those days of coarse thinking to notice the refinement and exquisite delicacy which pervade it; banishing every gross thought or immodest expression, and presenting womanly beauty in all its chivalrous qualities of almost supernatural purity and grace.

In 1424, on agreeing to pay a sum of £4,000, the poet-king was set at liberty. Returning to Scotland, he found the country given over to anarchy and rapine. "Let God but grant me life," he exclaimed, on realising its miserable condition, "and throughout my dominions I shall make the key keep the castle, and the bush secure the cow." The vigour with which he carried out a policy that was admirable in itself provoked a conspiracy against him, and he was murdered in the Dominican Monastery at Perth, on the 20th of February,

---

a Inlaid like fretwork. *b* Ruby. *c* Enamel. *d* Goldwork. *e* Fire or flame. *f* Match.

1436. Besides the "King's Quhair," he is reputed (but not on entirely satisfactory evidence) to have been the author of the satirical and humoristic poems of "Christ's Kirk on the Greene," and "Peebles to the Play."

One of the prisoners taken by Henry V. at Agincourt was Charles, Duke of Orleans. This accomplished prince had married Isabella of Valois, the young widow of Richard II., whom Henry IV. had eagerly endeavoured to secure as a bride for his own son; but their union lasted only for a few months, Isabella dying in September, 1310, in child-bed. At Agincourt he fought with desperate valour, and was left for dead on that disastrous field. Dragged from beneath a pile of the slain, the care of one Richard Waller, an English squire, restored him to life; but, on finding himself a prisoner, he was fain to refuse to eat or drink, and would have starved himself to death, but for the kindly attention of Henry V. The victor, however, rejected all offers of ransom, and the Duke was sent to England, where he was at first confined at Groombridge, and afterwards in the Tower. His captivity lasted for three-and-twenty years. He brightened it, as James I. had done, by cultivating the Muse, and composed those charming lays and lyrics which, to this day, are the delight of all elegant scholars. One of his graver efforts—an elegy on his wife Isabella—has been translated by Miss Strickland. It runs as follows:—

"To make my lady's obsequies,
My love a minster wrought,
And in the chantry service there
Was sung by doleful thought.
The tapers were of burning sighs
That life and odour gave;
And grief, illumined by tears,
Irradiated her grave :
And round about, in quaintest guise,
Was carved, "Within this tomb there lies
The fairest thing to mortal eyes."

"Above her lieth spread a tomb
Of gold and sapphires blue :
The gold doth show her blessèdness,
The sapphires mark her true;
For blessedness and truth in her
Were vividly portrayed!
When gracious God, with both His hands,
Her wondrous beauty made.
She was, to speak without disguise,
The fairest thing to mortal eyes.

"No more, no more; my heart doth faint,
When I the life recall
Of her who lived so free from taint,
So virtuous deem'd by all;

> Who in herself was so complete,
> I think that she was ta'en
> By God to deck His Paradise,
> And with His saints to reign ;
> For well she doth become the skies,
> Whom, while on earth each one did prize,
> The fairest thing to mortal eyes."

Part of the Duke's imprisonment, and doubtless the pleasantest part, was spent at Windsor.*

According to a well-established tradition, the victor of Agincourt had been warned, or his own astrological science had convinced him, that it would be dangerous for his first-born child to see the light at Windsor; and before setting out for France in June, 1421, he gave it in especial charge to Queen Katherine that her accouchement should take place elsewhere. For some reason, she thought proper to disobey her king and

WINDSOR CASTLE FROM THE PARK.

husband; and within the walls of royal Windsor, on the 6th of December, was born the unfortunate child who lived to wear the crown of England with the title of Henry VI. His father was conducting the siege of Meaux when the news reached him of the birth of a son. The legend records that he immediately asked, "Where was the boy

---

* * "Charles's life," says Mr. Hepworth Dixon, "is an epic of love and war, of glory and defeat, of suffering and resignation. Nature and events conspired to throw the conquering Henry and the captive Charles into opposite lists. Not only were they enemies in the field, but rivals in love. The Prince's father, Louis of Orleans, and the King's father, Henry of Lancaster, had each affected to consider himself heir to the crown of France; a splendid claim, which came down, in time, to their sons. Louis of Orleans, making himself the champion of a royal and unhappy lady, Isabella of Valois, Queen of England, widow of Richard the Second, had sent a challenge to Henry of Lancaster—as he contemptuously called the King of England—which Henry had declined with a cold and proud disdain. Louis called Henry a coward; Henry called Louis a fool. The young princes had both been in love with the 'fair woman,' as Shakespeare calls her— the widowed English queen, a daughter of Charles the Sixth—and Charles had carried away the prize. Henry was then our madcap Prince of Wales, the friend of Poins, the companion of Sir John. Charles was a poet, a musician, a courtier; and although Hal was of higher rank and riper age, Isabella had chosen the softer, more accomplished prince for her future mate. Rivals in ambition and in love, every turn in their fortunes helped to make English Henry dislike the young French prince."—*Her Majesty's Tower*, pp. 51, 52. The reader may also be referred to Mr. Lang's *Specimens of Early French Poetry*.

born?" and receiving for reply, "At Windsor," turned to Lord Fitzhugh, his chamberlain, muttering—

> "I, Henry, born at Monmouth,
> Shall small time reign, and much get;
> But Henry of Windsor shall long reign, and lose all of it,
> But, as God will, so be it."

The quatrain is prophetic and devout, but scarcely entitles Henry to a place in the catalogue of "Royal and Noble Authors." In her later years of suffering and sorrow, Katherine recalled her warrior-king's mysterious objection to Windsor, and became convinced that her disregard of it was the cause of the misfortunes of her son, Henry of Windsor.

Henry of Windsor did not die in the castle which witnessed his ill-omened birth, but he "sleeps his last sleep" in the vaults of St. George's Chapel. He was murdered in the Tower of London on the night of the 22nd of May, 1471, the day on which Queen Margaret had entered it as a prisoner. "But that the world," says Habington, "might not suspect that the king lived still, and thereupon be stirred up to new designs, he was no sooner dead, but with some show of funeral rites his body was brought into St. Paul's Church, where, upon Ascension Day, with his face uncovered, he was exposed to the curiosity of every eye. . . . From St. Paul's, next day, the corpse, obscurely, without any ceremony, was conveyed to the Black Friars, and from thence, by boat, to Chertsey in Surrey. Whence, after it had rested some while, it was removed to Windsor, and there at length found quiet." The removal took place because so many miracles were said to be wrought at the "sainted monarch's" tomb; and this odour of sanctity excited the jealousy of the Yorkist king. Henry's widow, "the lion-hearted Margaret," was for a short time imprisoned at Windsor.

To the splendid and luxurious Edward IV. we owe the erection of St. George's Chapel. He also enlarged and embellished the college of St. George, and richly endowed it, with the view of incorporating in it Henry VI.'s foundation of Eton. The chroniclers dwell with pleasure on the right royal state which he maintained in his "palace of Windsor;" and a graphic picture of it is furnished by Louis of Bruges, Lord of Granthuse, who visited him there in 1472.

On his arrival, he was conducted by Lord Hastings, the chamberlain, to "the far side of the quadrant," or quadrangle, to three chambers, then occupied by the king and queen. These apartments were sumptuously hung with cloth of gold arras. In one of them, Queen Elizabeth Woodville and her ladies were playing at the "Marteau," a game with balls like marbles; while others were amusing themselves with "closheys," or nine-pins of ivory, "which sight was full pleasant." Afterwards King Edward trod a measure with the Lady Elizabeth, his eldest daughter. Next morning, when matins were done, "the King heard, in his own Chapel, Our Lady mass, which was most melodiously sung." . . . Then Edward took his guest into the Little Park, where they had great sport, and the king made him ride on his own horse, "a right fair hobby," of which he afterwards made him a gift. Dinner was served in the lodge. Having recruited their strength, Edward and his guest were able to inspect the garden and "vineyard of pleasure," and this exercise fitted them to do their devoirs at a grand banquet which the queen ordained at her own apartments. There, "at one mess," sat the king and queen, their eldest daughter, the Duchess of Exeter, the Lady Rivers, and the Lord of Granthuse; at another table were placed the Duke of Buckingham—immortalised on the English stage by Colley Cibber's famous interpolation, "Off with his head; so much for Buckingham!"—the Duchess, the Lord Hastings—of whom Lord Lytton has drawn so favourable a portrait in his "Last of the Barons"—the Lord Berners—the son of Lord Granthuse, and Master George Barthe, secretary to the Duke of Burgundy. There was a side-table also, "at which sat a great *view* of ladies, all on one side of the room. Also, on one side of the outer chamber sat the queen's gentlewomen."

About nine o'clock, the King and Queen, with her ladies and gentlewomen, attended their guest to three "chambers of pleasaunce," all hanged with white silk and linen cloth, and the floors (it is specially noted) covered with carpets. "There was ordained a bed for himself, of as good down as could be gotten; the sheets of Rennes cloth. Also fine festoons; the counterpane, cloth of gold, furred with ermine. The tester and ceiler also shining cloth of gold, the curtains of white sarcenet; as for his head-suit and pillows, they were of the Queen's own ordering. In the second chamber was likewise another state-bed, all white. Also, in the chamber was made a couch with feather beds, and hanged above like a tent, knit like a net; and there was a cupboard. In the third chamber was ordained a *bain* (bath) or two, which were covered with tents of white cloth. And when the Queen, with all her ladies, had showed him these rooms, the Queen, with the King and attendants, turned again to their own chambers, and left the said Lord Granthuse there with the Lord Chamberlain Hastings, which despoiled him [helped him undress], and they both went together to the bath. And when they had been in their baths as long as was their pleasure, they had green ginger, divers syrups, comfits, and ipocras served by the order of the Queen. And in the morning he took his cup with the King and Queen, and returned to Westminster again."

Edward left express directions for his interment in St. George's Chapel, and his funeral was celebrated with great pomp. In 1492, his queen was placed by his side. She died in the convent of Bermondsey; and her body was conveyed by water to Windsor, with no other female attendant than one Mistress Greene, an illegitimate daughter of her husband's. It was Whit-Sunday, and at eleven o'clock the Queen's remains passed to their last resting-place. On the following Tuesday there was a gathering of kith and kin: her three daughters, Anne, Catherine, and Bridget, her nieces, the governess to her children, the Marquis of Dorset (her son by her first husband), her brother-in-law, and her son-in-law. That night began the dirge; but the Yorkist chronicler, who has transmitted these particulars to posterity, complains that but scant ceremony was observed, and the funeral

BURIAL OF EDWARD IV.

pageant seems to have been wofully deficient in dignity as well as splendour. In 1789 the vault where Edward and his queen lie buried was opened by certain officials. The King's body was found within a wooden coffin; the skeleton was entire, and measured six feet three inches. Another wooden coffin, much decayed, contained the skeleton of a woman, —undoubtedly that of the once beautiful Elizabeth Woodville :—

> "Thou, Elizabeth, art here—
> Thou to whom all griefs were known;
> Who wert placed upon the bier,
> In happier home than on a throne."

Henry VII. seems to have had a strong partiality for Windsor, and intended at one time to have erected in St. George's Chapel that magnificent mausoleum which is now one of the glories of Westminster Abbey. It was the scene of much pomp and pageantry in the reign of Henry VIII.; almost every day being marked by banquet or chase, or those knightly shows in which the young king, "the best rider, the best lance,

WINDSOR AT SUNRISE (FROM THE BROCAS).

and the best archer in England," bore so conspicuous a part. Notwithstanding the sumptuousness of his court, Henry does not appear to have been recklessly extravagant, his yearly expenditure not exceeding £19,894 16s. 8d., or about £250,000 of our money. He built the great gateway of the Lower Ward, and completed St. George's Chapel. In 1522, he was visited at Windsor by the Emperor Charles V. Ten years later, the ceremony of creating the fair Anne Boleyn Marchioness of Pembroke, as a step to her elevation to the throne, took place there. On Sunday, the 1st of September, the enamoured king, attended by the Dukes of Norfolk and Suffolk, the French ambassador, and a brave retinue of peers, entered the state-apartment, then called the "chamber of salutation," or the "presence-chamber," and seated his burly figure in the chair of state. Thither, conducted by a train of lords and ladies anxious to do homage to the royal favourite, came Anne Boleyn, a swarthy beauty, with bold, black eyes, large mouth, and long, but graceful neck. This was the order of procession: first, Garter-at-arms, in his gorgeously emblazoned tabard, bearing the King's patent of nobility. Next, the Lady Mary Howard, daughter to the Duke of Norfolk and cousin-german to Anne Boleyn, carrying on her left arm a robe of state, made of crimson velvet, trimmed with ermine, and in her right hand a coronet of gold. Then appeared the object of all this pageantry, Anne Boleyn herself, with her long black hair falling negligently about her face and rounded shoulders; she was attired in a surcoat of crimson velvet, lined with ermine, and with short sleeves; she walked between the Countess of Rutland and the Countess of Sussex, and was followed by many noble gentlewomen. As she approached the King's royal seat, she thrice made lowly obeisance; and on arriving before him, she kneeled. The patent having been presented to the King, he delivered it to his secretary, who read it aloud; and when he came to the words, "by putting on of a mantle" *(mantillæ inductionem)*, Henry took the robe of state from the Lady Mary, and threw it over Anne Boleyn's shoulders. At the words, "and the setting of a coronet of gold upon her head" *(circuli aurei)*, the Lady Mary handed him the coronet, which he placed on the brow of the newly-created Marchioness. When the charter had been read, he presented it to her, together with another that secured her a pension of £1,000 per annum for life, to enable her to uphold her dignity. She then thanked the King most humbly, and, looking triumphant in her robe and coronet, retired, the trumpets sounding a silver peal as she departed from the presence-chamber.

In the late autumn of 1540 Henry kept court at Windsor with his fifth wife, the fair and frail Katherine Howard. They remained about a month. In the following year they spent there four days in October, when the shadow of her coming doom was already impending over the unfortunate Queen. In February, 1547, the King's dead body was brought hither from Westminster to be buried, as directed in his will, in the choir of St. George's Chapel, "midway between the stalls and the high altar." A contemporary chronicler records a terrible incident as taking place on the funeral-route. "The King," he says, "being carried to Windsor to be buried, stood all night among the broken vales of Sein, and there the leaden coffin being cleft by the shaking of the carriage, the pavement of the church was wetted by his blood. In the morning came plumbers to solder the coffin, under whose feet—I tremble while I write it—was suddenly seen a dog creeping, and licking up the King's blood." The funeral sermon at Windsor was preached by Bishop Gardiner, from the text, "Blessed are the dead who die in the Lord." Then the corpse, being conveyed with great pomp to St. George's Chapel, was, when interred, let down into the vault by means of a vice, with the help of sixteen tall Yeomen of the Guard; the same bishop, standing at the head of the vault, proceded with the burial service; and when the mould was cast into the grave, at the words, "pulvis pulveri, cinis cineri," first the Lord Great-master, and after him the Lord Chamberlain and all the rest, broke their staves in shivers upon their heads, and cast them after the corpse into the pit, with exceeding sorrow and heaviness, not without grievous sighs and tears. Finally, the *De Profundis* was chanted, the grave covered over with planks, and Garter, attended by his officers, stood in the midst of the choir and proclaimed the young King's titles, and the rest of his officers repeated the same after him thrice. The ceremony concluded with the blast of trumpets, their silver sounds, it is said, "filling the hearts of those present with great comfort."

In 1566, while yet "Great Harry" was King, the poet-Earl of Surrey was imprisoned in the Castle, where he had formerly been the favourite playmate of Henry's natural son,

WINDSOR LASHER.

the Duke of Richmond. In one of his poems he enlarges, with characteristic sweetness of style, on the contrast between the *now* and the *then*:—

"So cruel prison how could betide, alas!
　　As proud Windsor, where I, in lust and joy,
　　With a King's son, my childish years did pass
　　In greater feast than Priam's son of Troy:

"Where each sweet place returns a taste full sour,
　　The large green courts where we were wont to hove,[a]
　　With eyes cast up into the Maiden Tower,
　　And easy sighs such as folks draw in love.

"The stately seats, the ladies bright of hue;
　　The dances short, long tales of great delight,
　　With words and looks that tigers could but rue,
　　When each of us did plead the other's right. . . .

"The gravel ground, with sleeves tied on the helm
　　Of foaming horse, with swords and friendly hearts;
　　With cheer as though one should another whelm,
　　Where we have fought, and chasèd oft with darts. . . .

"The wild forèst, the clothèd holts with green,
　　With reins availed,[b] and swift y-breathèd horse;
　　With cry of hounds and merry blasts between,
　　When we did chase the fearful hart of force."

---

a Hover about, or idle.　*b* Dropped.

After enumerating these and other pastimes which he had shared with his companion, a King's son, he falls into a strain of melancholy:—

" O, place of bliss! renewer of my woes,
    Give me accounts, where is my noble fere,[a]
Whom in thy walls thou dost each night enclose,—
    To others leef,[b] but unto me most dear?

" Echo, alas, that doth my sorrow rue,
    Returns thereto a hollow sound of plaint :
Thus I alone, where all my freedom grew,
    In prison pine with bondage and restraint,

" And with remembrance of the greater grief,
    To banish the less, I find my chief relief."

After a short captivity at Windsor, the Earl was released; but only to be re-arrested, and thrown into the Tower of London. He was tried by a common jury at Guildhall; found guilty of treason, because he had quartered on his shield the arms of Edward the Confessor; and was beheaded on the 21st of January, 1547.

a Comrade.   *b* Agreeable.

RUINS IN WINDSOR PARK

CHAPTER IX.
VIRGINIA WATER.

AMONG the places generally comprehended in a visit to Windsor is Virginia Water, though it lies nearly five miles to the south of the Castle, and is most conveniently approached from the Virginia Water Station of the London and South-Western Railway. It is royal property and enclosed, but admission is freely given to the public.

Virginia Water owes its existence to the good taste of a much maligned and greatly underrated man, William, Duke of Cumberland, the victor of Culloden, and uncle of George III. Having been appointed ranger of Windsor Great Park, he took up his residence, in 1746, in the house now known as Cumberland Lodge ("the Duke's Lodge," as Mrs. Delany calls it), a spacious and comfortable building, without architectural pretensions. He found at the southern end of the park a considerable stretch of marshy land, through which a streamlet slowly made its way to join the Thames at Chertsey. To provide the labourers of the neighbourhood with employment, and to improve the amenity of the Park, he resolved upon a somewhat extensive course of draining and planting, and, adopting the designs of Paul Sandby, the artist, proceeded to lay out Virginia Water.* The swamp was drained, the hollow deepened and enlarged, the stream dammed up, and the other watercourses of the neighbourhood diverted into the new basin. The borders were skilfully planted, and the outline was varied with much ingenuity, so as to prevent the actual dimension of the lake from being ascertained. The length does not exceed a mile and a-quarter, the maximum width one mile; but the design is so well carried out as to produce on the visitor an impression of much greater extent.

The dam gave way in 1768, and was rebuilt in a more substantial manner. At the same time was formed the waterfall, not one of the least agreeable characteristics of the scene, as it pours its shining silver through graceful plants and delicate green mosses and waving ferns. To the south of the Waterfall lies the Grotto, constructed of stones dug up at Bagshot Heath, and supposed to have belonged to a Druidical cromlech.

---

* So named in reference to the virgin wildernesses of the American colony, the more striking landscape features of which the artist boldly designed to reproduce.

Among the other curiosities, the Duke of Cumberland is responsible for the Chinese Pavilion and the Belvidere Fort; but George IV., who spent the last years of his life in the Royal Lodge, close at hand, is responsible for the Fishing Temple (rebuilt in 1875) and the Ruined Temple. The latter, composed of capitals, columns, and other architectural fragments originally brought from Greece and Tripoli, has been raised in a dark, moist dell, among fir and beech and a thick growth of bracken, and is cut in two by the bridge which crosses the Windsor and Blacknest road. There are also a boat-house, hermitage, floating bridge, and rustic bridge. The model man-of-war was placed on the lake by George IV.; the state barge, by Queen Victoria.

Virginia Water has been celebrated in verse by Charles Knight. He divides his poem into two parts, the cascade and the lake, and speaks of both in excellent taste and with accuracy of description. A little extra glow of imagination, however, seems to colour the following passage:—

> "I joy to know
> That tasteful memory doth dwell with thee;
> That temples, graceful as thy silent waters,
> Adorn thine islets; and that flowers as bright
> As stars, more sweet than flowers of Araby,
> Gleam 'midst thy willows. When the evening sun
> Glows in thy mirror, I may steal away
> From man's loud hum, to fancy that a note
> Of that soft music, clarionet and flute
> And mellow horn, that soothes a monarch's ear,
> Reaches my distant longings."

Still the scene is picturesque in the extreme; and dull, indeed, must be the fancy which derives no enjoyment from so graceful a combination of wood and water. The glimpses of luminous ripples through quaint frameworks of twisted boughs and drooping leaves, the loud babble of the mimic cascade, the thick fringe of wild flowers and pliant grasses, the general air of hush and repose, all add to the pleasing effect. There is "ample shade." There is the sweet softness of velvety lawns, which interpose their open spaces of air and light in the dark breadths of the woodland. There is a constant succession, as you move from point to point, of graceful and enchanting pictures. There is the music of birds, and the swift flight of wings across the dimpled glade. There is, in a word, everything to delight, to calm, to satisfy, and even to inspire.

Royal visits to Virginia Water are not so frequent now as they were of old. But it is not long since the Princess of Wales and her three daughters spent a summer evening here in agreeable fashion; rowing or sailing on the lake, and sauntering along its border. Afterwards they were joined by the Prince of Wales, and, with their suite, dined in the Fishing Cottage, once a favourite resort of George IV. A pleasanter spot for a royal picnic will scarcely be found in the "royal county!"

CHAPTER X.

WINDSOR: ITS LATER HISTORY.

THE BELL-TOWER—SATURDAY.

IT was at Windsor that Queen Mary celebrated, by a series of sumptuous entertainments, her marriage with Philip of Spain. The marriage itself took place at Winchester, in July; but the Queen hastened to show to her subjects the moody bridegroom for whom she dared and suffered so much. As they passed through London, says Mr. Green, men noted curiously the look of the young king, whose fortunes were interknit with those of England for nearly half-a-century. "Far younger than his bride, for he was but twenty-six, there was little of youth in the small and fragile frame, the sickly face, the sedentary habits, the Spanish silence and reserve, which estranged Englishmen from Philip, as they had already estranged his subjects in Italy, and his future subjects in the Netherlands."

As for Elizabeth, the Castle was very dear to her; she built the new gallery and banqueting-house; and, with a keen eye for the beautiful, constructed the North Terrace. There, in January, 1561, was represented before her the first English tragedy. It was constructed on the classic model, with choruses, by Sir Thomas Sackville (Lord Buckhurst) and Thomas Norton, and entitled "Ferrex and Porrex." The plot is founded on one of Geoffrey of Monmouth's stories, and is as full of blood and murder as a modern sensational novel. Elizabeth caused a stage to be erected for the regular performance of the drama, with painted scenes, properties, and dresses for the actors; while she provided an orchestra of trumpets and harps, viols, rebecks, and flutes, lutes, bagpipes, and sackbuts. She walked almost daily on her sunny promenade of the North Terrace, usually an hour before dinner, wet weather never preventing her, but wind always keeping her indoors. Sometimes she hunted in the neighbouring forest. A letter written by the Earl of Leicester to Archbishop Parker is extant, in which he says—"The Queen's Majesty being abroad hunting yesterday in the forest, and having had very good hap, beside great sport, she hath thought good to remember your Grace with part of her prey, and so commanded me to send you a great fog stag, killed with her own hand; which, because the weather was wet, and the deer somewhat chafed and dangerous to be carried so far without some help, I caused him to be parboiled for the better preservation of him, which I doubt not will cause him to come unto you as I would be glad he should."

In 1593, Shakespeare's comedy of the "Merry Wives of Windsor," written at her request, and, as an old tradition says, suggested by her hint that she would fain see the "fat knight" in love, was played before the Queen, probably in the New Gallery. At Windsor, in the same year, she translated the first five books of Boethius, on "The Consolations of Philosophy," in order to compose her mind after receiving the news of the perversion of Henry IV. of France to the Roman Church. Five years later, the German traveller, Hentzner, visited England, and Windsor <small>IRON LETTERS, NORTH WALK.</small> Castle was one of the places which most drew his admiration. He describes its three noble courts in glowing language, and especially the third court, in the centre of which flowed a fountain of the clearest water. Lavish is the praise he bestows upon the stately banqueting-hall; on the gallery, ornamented with figures and emblems, and the adjacent chamber, containing the royal beds of Henry VII. and his Queen, of Edward VI., Henry VIII., and Anne Boleyn, each

<small>LEAD WORK ON RAMPARTS, ROUND TOWER.</small>

eleven feet square, and covered by quilts that shone with gold and silver. The Queen's bed, not quite so long or large as the others, but embroidered with curious hangings of embroidery work, representing Clovis, King of France, presented by an angel with the fleur-de-lis

<small>LEAD WORK ON RAMPARTS, ROUND TOWER.</small>

as an heraldic device, was in the apartment in which Henry VI. was born. In the same apartment might be seen a table of red marble, streaked with white; a cushion elaborately wrought by Her Majesty's own august hands; "an unicorn's horn," upwards of eight spans and a-half in length, and valued at £10,000; and that wonder of the animal creation, which was then, indeed, a *rara avis* in Western Europe, a bird of Paradise. He also speaks of the terrace—" a walk of considerable beauty, three hundred and eighty paces in length, set round on every side with supporters of wood, which sustain a balcony, from whence the nobility and other persons of distinction can take the pleasure of seeing hunting and hawking in a lawn of sufficient space; for the fields and meadows, clad with a variety of plants and flowers, swell gradually into hills of perpetual verdure quite up to the castle, and at bottom stretch out into an extended plain that strikes the beholder with delight."

Hentzner draws a graphic portrait of the Queen at this date, when she was in her sixty-sixth year. She was, he says, very majestic; her face oblong, fair, but wrinkled; her eyes small, yet black and pleasant; her nose a little hooked, her lips narrow, and her teeth black. . . . She had in her ears two pearls, with very rich drops; she wore false hair, and that red; upon her head she had a small crown, reported to be made of some of the gold of the celebrated Lunebourg table. Her brow was uncovered, as all the English ladies have it till they marry; and she had on a necklace of exceeding fine jewels. Her hands were small, her fingers long, and her stature neither tall nor low; her air was stately, her manner of speaking mild and obliging. That day she was dressed in white silk, bordered with pearls of the size of beans, and over it a mantle of black silk, shot with silver threads; her train was very long, the end of it borne by a marchioness. Attended by the ladies of the court, all handsome and well-shaped, and guarded by the gentlemen pensioners, one hundred and seventy-eight in number, with gilded battle-axes, she went on her way, amid shouts of "Long live Queen Elizabeth," the cynosure of every eye,—

"A virgin queen, attired in white."

A characteristic anecdote of Elizabeth has Windsor for its *locale*. When her Majesty removed from one of her palaces to another, as was her frequent custom, all the carts and horses in the neighbourhood, with their drivers, were "requisitioned" for the transport of her luggage. A carter was once ordered to come to the Castle for this purpose; but when he came the Queen had altered the day. A second time he came in vain. He obeyed a third summons; but, after waiting some hours, was told that "the remove did not hold." Clapping his hand on his thigh, the sturdy varlet exclaimed, "Now I see that the Queen is a woman as well as my wife." This bold speech being overheard by Elizabeth, as she stood near an open window, she exclaimed, "What villain is this!" and sent him three angels to stop his mouth, and compensate, we suppose, for his loss of time.

But she was now growing old; the sun which had risen above the horizon with so much splendour was slowly sinking in cloud and shadow. Still she fought against Time with all the courage of her race. She hunted in Windsor Forest; she jested with her favourites; she gave banquets; she danced and she coquetted and she frolicked at sixty-seven as at twenty-seven. Only a few months before her death, a courtier wrote—"The Queen was never so gallant these many years, nor so set upon jollity." She did not cease, however, to keep in her own hands the reins of government; to receive foreign ambassadors; to hold council with her statesmen, though she had outlived the old generation, the Burleighs and the Walsinghams, who had served her so well and so devotedly, and the new school turned their eyes towards the king that was to be, the "Solomon of the North." The days passed by—weary days to that aged queen and lonely woman—and the shadow of death drew visibly nearer. A singular melancholy oppressed her; the result, perhaps, of her inwardly contrasting what she had been with what she was. Gradually her strong intellect gave way. Her memory was obviously impaired; the violence of her tongue became intolerable; her very courage seemed to abandon her. "She called for a sword to lie constantly beside her, and thrust it from time to time through the arras, as if she heard murderers stirring there. Food and rest were alike distasteful. She sat night and day propped up with pillows on a stool, her finger on her lip, her eyes fixed on the floor, without a word. If she once broke the silence, it was with a flash of her old queenliness. When Robert Cecil declared that she 'must' go to bed, the word roused her like a trumpet. 'Must!' she exclaimed; 'is *must* a word to be addressed to princes? Little man, little man! thy father, if he had been alive, durst not have used that word.' Then, as her anger spent itself, she sank into her old dejection. 'Thou art so presumptuous,' she said, 'because thou knowest I shall die.' She rallied once more when the ministers beside her bed named Lord Beauchamp, the heir to the Suffolk claim, as a possible successor. 'I will have no rogue's son,' she cried hoarsely, 'to sit in my seat.' But she gave no sign, save a motion of the hand, at the mention of the King of Scots. She was in fact fast becoming insensible; and early the next morning, on the 24th of March, 1603, the life of Elizabeth, a life so great, so strange and lonely in its greatness, ebbed quietly away."

Elizabeth's last days were spent at Whitehall; but among the noble figures which seem to crowd around us as we tread the halls and corridors of the royal Castle, hers, in its queenly dignity, and with its "lion port," is one of the most conspicuous.

James I. was a constant resident at Windsor, hunting in the Forest, and giving frequent entertainments in the Castle; where, in September, 1621, Ben Jonson's masque of "the Metamorphosed Gipsies" was acted before him. Numerous, too, are the souvenirs of Charles I. which attach to the ancient palace. He was here with his beautiful bride, Henrietta Maria, shortly after their marriage; and here he spent his last and most sorrowful Christmas, after his removal from Carisbrooke, in the Isle of Wight. His residence on this occasion extended over a month. On the 15th of January he left it for the last time. His kinsman, the Duke of Hamilton, who was also a prisoner there, had bribed his gaolers to permit him a farewell interview; and, escorted by his guards, intercepted him as he passed forth. Flinging himself on his knees, he exclaimed, " My dear, dear master!" but could say no more. " I have indeed been a *dear* master to you," replied the King, affectionately embracing him. After that tragedy at Whitehall, which so many condemn, and few excuse, while all pity, the body was removed to Windsor, with an escort of four mourning coaches, and placed, for the night, in the royal bedchamber. The next day it was conveyed into St. George's Hall; the coffin being borne on the shoulders of four gentlemen formerly belonging to the King's household, who were clad in deepest mourning, while the pall was supported by the Duke of Richmond, the Earl of Hertford, and the Lords Lindsay and Southampton. Bright and sunny had been the afternoon till the corpse was carried out of the Hall; then the snow began to fall, and it fell so swiftly and so heavily, that by the time it reached the west end of the royal chapel, the black velvet pall was entirely white, " the colour of innocency." " So went our white King to his grave," said Charles's sorrowing attendants. Bishop Juxon, with open prayer-book, met the procession at the chapel-door, and was about to read the Anglican funeral service, when he was checked by the puritan Whichcott, then governor of the Castle. At the last moment it was discovered that the coffin bore no inscription; whereupon a strip of sheet-lead was procured; the gentlemen present cut out in it, in large letters, the words and date, "CHARLES REX, 1648," and firmly bound it about the coffin. Still thickly fell the snow; the gloom of a winter night fast gathered over the scene; and so, "without either singing or saying," but with the tribute of many tears, lowered his remains among the dead King's faithful servants dust of his predecessors.

In the reign of Charles II., Windsor underwent considerable renovation and enlargement, the new buildings being designed by Sir Christopher Wren, but in a style as unworthy of his genius as of the royal castle. The most important was named the Star Building, from a carved star of the order of the Garter on its northern façade. Charles, when at Windsor, indulged to his heart's content in his favourite exercise of walking, and frequently hunted the stag in the neighbouring forest. In the decoration of the interior he employed Grinling Gibbons, beneath whose touch wood became plastic as wax; and "sprawling" Verrio, with his passion for grotesque allegory; while Sir Peter Lely was ordered to paint for the

STONE WORK ON RAMPARTS, ROUND TOWER.

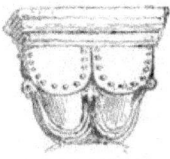
CAPITAL ON RAMPARTS, ROUND TOWER.

King's own apartments those portraits of the Beauties of his Court ("whose drapery hints we may admire them freely") now preserved at Hampton. The haughty Castlemaine, the reserved Frances Stewart, the seductive Louise de Querouaille, all paraded their loveliness in Windsor's splendid halls.

CAPITAL ON RAMPARTS, ROUND TOWER.

It was at Windsor, in 1687, that James II. received the Papal Envoy,* and provoked the public indignation by putting up a Roman Catholic Chapel, where he and his Queen ostentatiously heard mass. His successor, William of Orange, "the Deliverer," preferred Hampton Court to the ancient residence of the English Kings; but he carried out the works which Charles II. had begun, and ordered the construction of "the Long Walk." He also entertained the unhappy design of converting the grand old pile into a semi-classical palace, after the modern fashion, but, fortunately, it never went beyond a conception.

Queen Anne was partial to Windsor, and every year spent there a considerable portion of her time. Her affection for it dated probably from the period when William III. first placed it at her disposal (in 1696) as a summer abode, confining KNOCKER AT NO. 10 CLOISTER. himself to the quasi-Dutch paradise which he had created at Hampton Court. On removing thither, the Princess appropriated a suite of apartments to the use of her son, the young Duke of Gloucester, and it is said that

---

* It was the Duke of Somerset's duty, as first lord of the bedchamber, to introduce the Nuncio; but he refused, saying that it was contrary to the law. "Do you not know that I am above the law?" said James. "But I am not," calmly replied the Duke.

the martial young prince, on being conducted through them, complained that his presence-chamber was not large enough for him to exercise his soldiers in it. His cicerone, on this occasion, was the housekeeper, a Mrs. Randes, who dilated on the various objects of interest the castle contained, and described the subjects of the pictures. He seems to have been especially pleased with Andrea Mantegna's "historical picture of the Triumph in St. George's Hall;" and declared that that splendid apartment was just the place for him and his soldiers to fight their mimic battles in. The next day four Eton boys arrived to be his playmates and companions; the two Bathursts, Peter Boscawen, and young Lord Churchill, son of the great Marlborough. The Duke immediately suggested that they should perform a grand feat-of-arms in St. George's Hall, and sent for his private arsenal of muskets, swords, and pikes. It was agreed that the music gallery should represent a castle, which was to be duly besieged and defended. The lady and gentleman-in-waiting were both called upon to engage in the fray, and it is recorded that they begged young Boscawen to take the part of "the enemy," as he was a youth of prudence and quiet temper, who would be careful not to injure the Duke with the military weapons. One of the Bathursts proved to be less discreet, and the sheath having slipped off his sword, he gave the Duke a wound in the neck that bled. While the battle raged, the courageous boy said nothing of the accident; but the equerry stopped to inquire if he was hurt. "No," exclaimed the chivalrous young paladin, and hotly pressed the defenders in their garrison, "leaving the floor of St. George's Hall strewed with make-believe dying and dead." When the fight was over, he asked Mrs. Atkinson if a surgeon were in attendance. "Oh yes, sir," she replied; for it was the custom in the Prince's sham-battles to revive the dead by blowing wind into them with a pair of bellows. "Pray make no jest of it," rejoined the Duke, "for Peter Bathurst has really wounded me." The wound, however, was light enough; and the young Prince (he was only seven years old) was taken in the afternoon to see the Round Tower. He objected to it that it had neither parapet nor bastion.

The ranger of the Park presented the Prince with a buck, to kill as he pleased. His governor, however, would not allow him to have it hunted, and it was slaughtered in a manner far from edifying. The deer was wounded and disabled before being turned out by the keeper, and the Duke followed the pursuit in his coach, while young Boscawen, on horseback, contrived to intercept the maimed creature, turned it towards the coach, and cut its throat in the young Duke's presence, that he might have "say" in the first sight of the death of a buck. Mr. Marlowe, his page, dipped his hand in the blood, with which he besmeared his highness's face. At first he was a little startled, but on being told that such was the custom at first seeing a deer slain, he hastened, with much glee, to bedaub his usher, and afterwards his playfellows. The whole cortege, then, by his desire, wound their way home under the windows of his mother's apartments, and saluted her with the orthodox "halloo." He would fain have given "the say" to those of her ladies who had never seen a deer slaughtered, but they did not care to have their faces painted of so sanguine a complexion.

WINDSOR CASTLE

The boy's birthday was on the 24th of July, and on that day King William held a Chapter of the Knights of the Garter, in St. George's Hall, for the admission of the young Duke. We are told that the banquet and procession were on a scale of unusual splendour, and that the boy-knight behaved with a dignity and a seriousness that made him the observed of all observers. His noble knights-companions were his father, Prince George of Denmark, the Dukes of Devonshire, Norfolk, Northumberland, Shrewsbury, and Southampton, and the Earls of Dorset and Rochester. All the knights dined in full panoply, and the little Duke with them, but after he had been at table a while, and had partaken of some refreshment, he asked leave to retire. His mother wisely ordered him to lie down and rest himself, and when he had slept for two or three hours, she took him out in her carriage for an airing. In the evening the Princess received a great gathering of the nobility, many of whom came from a distance to pay their respects and be present at the magnificent ball which closed the day's festivities. Windsor was illuminated; the bells of all the surrounding church-towers rang forth their merriest peals; and the neighbouring hills blazed with huge bonfires. A grand display of fireworks took place on the castle-lawn, and it is probable that no part of the proceedings was witnessed by the Duke with more delight.

On the anniversary of his mother's wedding-day, he superintended the firing of his little artillery in her honour. He was the proud possessor of four miniature cannon, three of which had been made for him by order of his aunt, Queen Mary, while the fourth was a beautiful model, the work of that hero-cavalier, Prince Rupert. On entering her son's room the Princess was saluted with a "volley of

THE CLOISTERS ABOVE THE STEPS.

ordnance" (as the old writers have it), but as he indulged in three rounds, his anxious mother felt some alarm at his having so much gunpowder in his possession, and privately resolved to limit the supply. Having finished his military duties, he addressed his parents with much vivacity. "Papa," he said, "I wish you and Mamma 'unity, peace, and concord,' not for a time, but for ever." His usher, who has handed down to posterity all these details, afterwards observed, "You made a fine compliment to their Royal Highnesses to-day, sir." "Lewis," he replied, "it was no compliment; it was sincere." "He now,"

L

adds the usher, "though he had but completed his seventh year, began to be more wary in what he said, and would not talk and chatter just what came into his head, but now and then would utter shrewd expressions with some archness."

The Duke's eleventh birthday was celebrated at Windsor (in 1700) with the usual rejoicings. He reviewed his regiment of juvenile warriors, made "the welkin ring" with cannon and crackers, and presided at a superb banquet. The heat and fatigue, however, added, perhaps, to unaccustomed indulgence in the luxuries of the table, proved too much for him, and next day he complained of headache, sickness, and a sore throat. Towards night, delirium came on. He was bled, according to the sanguinary practice of the time, but his condition did not improve, and Dr. Radcliffe, the celebrated physician, was sent for. As soon as he saw the patient, he pronounced that his malady was scarlet fever. "Who bled him?" he angrily demanded; and when the physician in attendance owned that he was responsible, "You have destroyed him," he exclaimed, "and you may finish him, for I will not prescribe." This prediction proved only too true; the young prince, who was unquestionably a lad of high promise, died on the 30th of July. His remains were conveyed to London, and, on the 9th of August, solemnly interred in Westminster Abbey, in the vault near Henry VII.'s Chapel.

This melancholy event appears to have intensified Anne's liking for royal Windsor. Soon after her accession to the throne, we read that she retired to Windsor. One of her earliest acts as Queen was to appoint her favourite, "Mrs. Morley," Keeper of Windsor Park;* and Windsor was the scene of the backstair intrigues and closet cabals that resulted in the Duchess's downfall, and the substitution of Mrs. Masham as confidential attendant. It was here that Mrs. Masham frequently entertained her royal mistress by playing on the harpsichord, and singing very agreeably. Here, in 1703, the Queen received Charles of Austria, then a candidate for the throne of Spain. The Prince-Consort had escorted him thither from Petworth, in Sussex, the splendid seat of the Duke of Somerset; and it affords a striking illustration of the difficulties of locomotion in those days, that the Prince occupied fourteen hours in the journey! He and his guest arrived at Windsor on the night of the 29th of December, and was received by torch-light. The lord-chamberlain conducted the King-expectant to the stair-head, where he was welcomed by the Queen. The same night royalty supped in state, Charles sitting on the Queen's right hand. Ceremonialism was rampant throughout the royal Austrian's stay; but the particulars would interest none but heralds and court-chamberlains.

Anne was at Windsor, and seated in her royal closet, which commanded a splendid prospect over the north terrace, when the glorious tidings arrived of the great victory of Blenheim. For several years the banner by which, in memory of this decisive battle, the Duke of Marlborough holds the manor of Woodstock, was appropriately deposited in this

---

* "The Queen was pleased to give me," wrote her Grace of Marlborough afterwards, "as soon as she came to the Crown, the rangership of the Great and Little Parks at Windsor. The house is an agreeable place to live in, and Her Majesty was pleased to give it to me herself, remembering that, when she was Princess, I had wished mightily for such a lodge, as we rid by it to take the air."

apartment. It forms, we are told, a kind of boudoir or ante-chamber to one of the state bedchambers, where, in an alcove, is still preserved the Queen's ponderous embroidered bed—a bed huge and heavy as the bed of Ware, which is still to be seen in the gardens of the Rye House on the river Lea. The daily routine of Anne's life at Windsor may be briefly indicated. The bedchamber woman (Mrs. Masham) made her appearance before the Queen's prayers; and as soon as she rose, if any lady of the bedchamber was present, the bedchamber woman handed her the royal linen, and the lady put it on her Majesty. Whenever the Queen dressed, the same tedious formality was observed. The Queen washed her hands; her page of the backstairs setting upon a side-

THE THRONE ROOM, WINDSOR.

table a bason or ewer. The bedchamber woman placed it before her Majesty, and knelt on the other side of the bath, while the lady of the bedchamber looked on. The bedchamber woman poured the water out of the ewer on the royal hands, and afterwards, when the Queen was disabled by gout, pulled on the royal gloves. The page of the backstairs was always called to put on the Queen's shoes. When she dined in public, her page handed the glass to her bedchamber woman, and she passed it to the lady-in-waiting. After a troublesome transit, it happily washed the lips of Majesty. The bedchamber woman, after dinner, brought the Queen chocolate, and in her private chamber the Queen enjoyed a little *siesta*. The royal dinner-hour was three punctually, and at six the Queen held her council, and received her ministers. The evening was generally concluded with a game of cards.

Balls and banquets were also of frequent occurrence and, on the whole, her Majesty's sojourn at Windsor must have been the pleasantest of her young experiences. The last days of her invalid Consort, Prince George of Denmark (the "*Est-il-possible?*" of the history of the Revolution), were spent among the leafy shades of Windsor, not at the Castle, but at a small house or lodge in the forest, which Anne had purchased before her accession to the throne. She was there, in affectionate attendance upon him, when she received the news of the victory of Oudenarde. "Oh, Lord!" she exclaimed, with a touch of womanly sympathy, "when will all this dreadful bloodshed cease?" Shortly afterwards, she removed Prince George to Kensington, where he died on the 28th of October. Anne immediately retired to Windsor, to grieve over her loss.

Sovereigns have little time to mourn: and the widowed Queen was soon called upon to resume the usual routine of laborious duties and formal pleasures; to contend with her imperious Grace of Marlborough; to make her customary journeys from St. James's to Hampton Court, and Hampton Court to Windsor; and to arbitrate as best she could between rival place-hunters and politicians. Dean Swift, writing to Stella (Hester Johnson) in July, 1711, notes that "the Queen was abroad to-day to hunt, but finding it disposed to rain, she kept in her coach. She hunts in a chaise with one horse, which she drives herself, and drives furiously like Jehu, and is a mighty hunter like Nimrod." A week later, she hunted the stag through the hot hours of the day until four in the afternoon, driving full forty miles; and yet she was not too fatigued on the following day to hold a drawing-room. It was but scantily attended, however; and so "her Majesty," says Swift, "sent for us into her bedchamber, where we made our bows, and stood, about twenty of us, round the room, while she looked at us, with her fan in her mouth, and once a minute said two or three words to some that were nearest to her, and then, being told dinner was ready, went out." Why does not some great humorous painter reproduce for us this dramatic scene of the British Sovereign surveying the lords and ladies who had come to do her homage, *with her fan in her mouth?* "I dined," continues Swift, "at her Majesty's board of green cloth. . . . It is much the best table in England, and costs the Queen a thousand pounds a-month while she is at Windsor or Hampton Court, and is the only mark of magnificence or royal hospitality that I can see in the Queen's household. It is designed to entertain foreign ministers and people of quality, who come to see the Queen, and have no place to dine." In taking leave of the cynical Dean, we may note that one of the bitterest of his lampoons is entitled "The Windsor Prophecy," written in the interest of Mrs. Masham and the Tory ministry.

In the autumn of 1712, while at Windsor, Queen Anne was attacked by an intermittent fever, which at that time raged in the royal household, no fewer than forty persons suffering from it. Its ill effects on the Queen's health were permanent, and thenceforth she was compelled to give up the long hunting-drives in which she had previously delighted. Her accesses of gout were more frequent and prolonged; her obesity increased; and as she could neither ascend nor descend the castle stairs without difficulty, or indeed danger, she was lowered from one room into another by means of a chair fitted up with pulleys and tackling. Her court poet and jester, Tom D'Urfy, was at this time abusing the Electress Sophia in doggrel ryhmes :—

> "The crown's far too weighty
> For shoulders of eighty,
> She could not sustain such a trophy;
> The hand, too, already
> Has grown so unsteady
> She can't hold a sceptre—
> So Providence kept her
> Away, poor old dowager Sophy!"

but many of his readers must have felt that the satire might be retorted upon Queen Anne herself.

The first two Georges seldom visited the Castle ; and George III. and his family, on taking up their residence at Windsor, built for their better accommodation "the Queen's Lodge," where they lived in that plain and homely style which secured for the "farmer King" so great a popularity. On Sunday afternoon they paraded the terrace, attended by their court; state ceremonial being absolutely eschewed, and the public freely allowed to breathe the air of royalty. When not *en évidence*, however, Queen Charlotte seems to have maintained, if Miss Burney's lively pages may be believed, a considerable amount of etiquette; and her maids of honour, whether at Windsor, at Kew, or at St. James's, led no easy life. Whether well or ill, Miss Burney was required to rise and dress very early, that, at half-past seven, she might answer the royal bell. For half-an-hour (as we have elsewhere written) it was her proud privilege to attend in the Queen's dressing-room, to lace the royal stays, and put on the royal hoops, gown, and neck-handkerchief. The morning was occupied in finding a place for everything, and putting everything—especially the royal finery—in its place. Afterwards, the Queen had to be powdered and dressed ; and twice a-day the royal hair had to be curled and *crêped* after the monstrous fashion of the times, the process consuming some twenty minutes. About three, Frances was dismissed, and she could then count on a couple of hours for herself. At five, she had to wait upon Madame Schellenberg, her colleague, or we should rather say, *gouvernante*, a woman of despotic and querulous temper, who, despising literature, and jealous of Miss Burney's renown, gratified a mean spirit of revenge by heaping upon her continual insults. How the unfortunate maid-of-honour rejoiced when, soon after eleven, the bell rang for her to attend the Queen, and assist in the elaborate operation of undressing. Five years of this servitude broke down Miss Burney's health, and yet she was afraid to resign her post. Her friends represented to her father the urgent need that existed for withdrawing her from it; and though he could hardly conceive of anything more exalted or gratifying than to live in the constant presence, as it were, of the King and Queen, he was induced, at last, to promise to interfere. But he showed an extraordinary dilatoriness in redeeming his promise ; and meanwhile his daughter grew paler, she suffered from breathlessness, tremblings, and sharp pains in the sides. She took bark, and she took wine, and she took opium, for the doctors at one time prescribed tonics, and at another stimulants; but in vain. Three or four times in an evening she was compelled to quit the card-table, and crawl to her own room, that by doses of hartshorn she might keep herself from fainting. Again her friends came to the rescue, and beset her father with importunities and reproaches. Boswell obtained an interview with the martyr herself at the choir gate of St. George's Chapel. "I am very glad to see you," he exclaimed, "but very sorry to see you here. My dear ma'am, why do you stay?—it won't do, ma'am, you must resign." And eventually she *did* resign; taking her leave of the Queen on the 7th of July, 1791, and retiring into privacy to finish that agreeable "Diary" which furnishes such graphic pictures of English Court-life in the days when George III. was king.

In Mrs. Delany's autobiography will be found some interesting sketches of Windsor at the time we speak of; of the Sunday promenades on the Terrace, and the stirring strains of two military bands, and the pleased countenances of the crowd, and the inner groups of naval and military officers, politicians, and clerical dignitaries, and the duteous bows and curtseys of the "loyal lieges," as George, with his ill-favoured queen, and train of princes and princesses, moved up and down "amidst the double line."

Mrs. Delany gives an interesting sketch of the "surroundings" of the Castle in 1757. Driving through the great park, she went, she says, to the Duke's Lodge, which she describes as a "bad house, not worth seeing." It was being repaired and enlarged. "The improvements about it (which they call the garden) consist of broad walks—some winding, some straight; on one side planted with flowering shrubs, the other side only scattering old trees, formerly an hedgerow, but now opened for the prospect of the country, which is very fine. The menagerie is not stored with great variety, but great quantities of Indian pheasants, the gold kind, blue and white, and the common sort. The wild and foreign beasts are all sent to the Tower."

She goes on to tell of "a terrible accident" that had occurred there not very long before. The tiger escaped from his den, and tore a boy of eight or nine years of age to pieces; the mother was standing by; she rushed upon the beast, and thrust her hands and arms into its very jaws to save her child. The keeper got her away safely, but the poor lad perished. After this misfortune, the Duke sent his "wild and foreign beasts" to the Tower as the only fitting place for them. "There is a dromedary—an ugly creature; it is kept in a yard by itself. It made a hideous noise, and frightened the horses."

Mrs. Delany continues:—"About half-a-mile from the place we took coach at, we came to a very pretty bridge and piece of water, but not worth mentioning in comparison of what we saw about a mile from thence—which is the piece of water and bridge so much talked of—and more cannot be said than it deserves. On the water is a Chinese vessel called "the Mandarin," as rich and gay as carving, gilding, and japanning can make it; it stands on the middle of the lake, and we went to it in a boat. From thence we went to the Tower on Shrub Hill, which is at one end of the piece of water, a little distance from it, and overlooks all the improvements. It is built in a triangular form, at each corner a square or octagon turret; one of them is the winding stone staircase that leads to the great room (which is hexagon); the other two are closets, one painted and carved (blue and gold), with shelves filled with books, the other gold and green, with shelves filled with china; the middle room in stucco, adorned with hanging festoons of fruits and flowers painted in their natural colours, the ground white; in the middle hangs a lustre of Chelsea china that cost six hundred pounds, and is really beautiful. Nothing can be finer than the prospects from all the windows. The hill on which the Tower stands is laid out in winding walks, and planted with an infinite variety of shrubs."

Let us take next a picture of a royal stag-hunt, followed by a sketch of a Windsor interior:—" On Wednesday morning, a quarter before ten, the Duchess of Portland stepped into her chaise, and we went to Gerard's Cross, about the middle of the Common, by the appointment and command of the King, who came about a quarter of an hour after, with the Prince of Wales and a large retinue. His Majesty came up immediately to the Duchess of Portland's carriage, most gracious, and delighted to see the Duchess out so early; the Queen was there, with the two eldest Princesses, and Lady Wintoun in a post-coach and four; the King came with a message from the Queen to the Duchess of Portland, to say that she would see her safe back to Bulstrode, to breakfast with her Grace. The Duke of Cumberland was there; a great many carriages, and many of our acquaintance, amongst them Lady Mary Forbes and her family, who took three rooms at the Bull Inn, and breakfasted thirty people; the King himself ordered the spot where the Duchess of Portland's chaise should stand to see the stag turned out; it was brought in a cart to that place. At the King's command the stag was set at liberty, and the poor trembling creature bounded over the plain in hopes of escaping from his pursuers, but the dogs and the hunters were soon after him, and all out of sight. The Duchess of Portland returned home in order to be ready to receive the Queen, who immediately followed before we could pull off our cloaks! We received her Majesty and the Princesses on the steps at the door, but she is so gracious that she makes everything perfectly easy. We got home a quarter before eleven, and the Queen stayed till two. In her return back to Windsor she met the chase, and was at the taking of the stag; but they would not let the dogs kill him.

"On Wednesday the Duchess intended to go to return the Queen thanks for the honour she had done her. We were to set out early; Ria got up in her sleep, and I dressed my head for the day before breakfast, when a letter came from Miss Hamilton from the Queen's Lodge to me with a message from the King, to desire we would not come till Thursday evening at eight o'clock, as he could not be at home until then. Accordingly we went; were there at the appointed hour; the King and Queen and Princesses received us in the drawing-room, to which we went through the concert-room. Princess Mary took me by the left hand, Princess Sophia and the dear little Prince Octavius by the right hand, and led me after the Duchess of Portland into the drawing-room; the King nodded and smiled upon my little conductors, and bid them lead me up to the Queen, who stood in the middle of the room. When we were all seated (for the Queen is so gracious she always makes me sit down), the Duchess of Portland sat next to the Queen. I sat next to the Princess Royal ; on the other side of me was a chair, and his Majesty did me the honour to sit by me ; he went backwards and forwards between that and the music-room, and he was so good as to have a good deal of conversation with me, particularly about Handel's music, and ordered those pieces to be played which he found I had a preference for. In the course of the evening the Queen changed places with the Princess Royal, saying graciously she 'must have a little conversation with Mrs. Delany,' which lasted about half-an-hour ; she then got up, it being half-an-hour after ten, and said she was afraid she should keep the Duchess of Portland too late, and made her curtsey, and we withdrew. There was nobody there but the attendants and Lord and Lady Wintoun, and nothing could be more agreeable. We came home very well lighted by our lanterns and the Northern Lights, sat down and ate supper at twelve o'clock, and slept very well after it."

HORSE SHOE CLOISTERS.

The reader may not be displeased with another of these domestic sketches. Mrs. Delany, it appears, was appointed " to go to the lodge at Windsor at two o'clock. We were first taken," she says, " into the Duchess of Ancaster's dressing-room ; in a quarter of an hour after to the King and Queen in the drawing-room, who had nobody with them but the Prince Alverstaden, the Hanoverian minister, which gave me an opportunity of hearing the Queen speak German, and I may say it was the *first* time I had received pleasure from what I did not understand, but there was such a fluency and sweetness in her manner of speaking it, *that it sounded as gentle as Italian !*" How marvellous is the influence of a queen's voice!

"There were two chairs brought in for the Duchess of Portland and myself to sit on (by order of their Majesties), which were easier chairs than those belonging to the room. We were seated near the door that opened to the concert room. The King directed them to play Handel and Geminiani's music, which he was pleased to say was to gratify me.

These are flattering honours, and I should not indulge so much upon this subject, but that I depend upon your believing it proceeds more from gratitude than vanity. The three eldest princesses came into the room in about half-an-hour after we were seated. All the royal family were dressed in a uniform for the *demi-saison* of a violet blue armozine with gauze aprons, etc., etc. The Queen had the addition of a great many fine pearls.

"When the concert of music was over, the young Princess Amelia, nine weeks old, was sent for, and brought in by her nurse and attendants. The King took her in his arms, and presented her to the Duchess of Portland and to me. Your affectionate heart would have been delighted with this royal domestic scene."

Charles Knight informs us that, on one occasion, he saw no less illustrious an individual than William Pitt waiting among the crowd until his royal master and mistress should issue forth, and descend the steps leading to the Eastern Terrace. George III. made some additions to the Castle, and "restored" St. George's Chapel, under the superintendence of James Wyatt; but Wyatt's work was deplorably bad, and scarcely any of it now remains.

It is scarcely an exaggeration to speak of George IV. as the second founder of Windsor. In 1823 he conceived the idea of remodelling and enlarging its ancient and incongruous buildings, so as to convert them into a fit residence for an English sovereign; and he obtained from Parliament a grant of £300,000 for this purpose. The architect chosen was Mr. Jeffry Wyatt, afterwards knighted as Sir Jeffry Wyatt-

ST. GEORGE'S CHAPEL, WEST END.

ville, who took up his abode in the Castle, and devoted himself, until his death in 1840, to his difficult and laborious undertaking. The royal apartments were completed, and taken possession of by the King, in 1828; but the work of reconstruction went on until the entire eastern half of the Castle was renewed, and a generally harmonious character impressed upon the different portions of the vast pile. The total cost exceeded a million pounds. It is easy, no doubt, for the critic to find fault with the details. Sir Jeffry lived before the age of Pugin, Ruskin, and Gilbert Scott. But it can hardly be denied that to him and his royal patron we are indebted for one of the finest palaces in Europe; one which may be surpassed, perhaps, in magnificence, but is unequalled in picturesqueness of effect.

The necessary enlargement of the superficial area was obtained chiefly within the quadrangle, on the exterior facing the North Terrace, to which the Brunswick Tower was added; also, "by converting what was two open courts in that northern mass of building, namely, the Brick Court and Stone Court, into the State Staircase and the Waterloo Gallery. A splendid corridor, 450 feet in length, was designed, so as to provide separate access to rooms which had previously opened into one another. Several apartments were united, so as to obtain sufficient space for state ceremonials; and additional public and private rooms were built. The Waterloo Gallery was constructed, and St. George's Hall enlarged. Externally, new towers were erected, and old ones elevated; a certain uniformity of aspect was carefully studied; and an air of dignity was given to the whole fabric by the increased height of the Round Tower, which, from the level of the Quadrangle, now rises to a total altitude of 148 feet.

Such associations as connect George IV. with Windsor, belong, however, to the Royal Lodge, rather than to the Castle, which he so sumptuously reconstructed. In the closing months of his life he abandoned the Castle, and, in his nervous dread of publicity, withdrew to the seclusion of the Great Park. Here his favourite amusement was to make war against the fish of Virginia Water, in company with the Marchioness of Conyngham, who had obtained a powerful influence over his enfeebled mind. He found it hard work, poor man! to kill time, though he must have known that few were the days remaining to him; and Mr. Greville's "Diary," as well as other chronicles, presents a painful picture of his morbid restlessness, his irritability, his fits of despondency, and his gradual intellectual decay. "He was very fond of punch," writes Captain Gronow, "made from a recipe of his *maître d'hôtel*, and which he drank after dinner. This was the only time he was agreeable, and on these occasions he would sing songs, relate anecdotes of his youth, and play on the violoncello, afterwards going to bed in a 'comfortable' state. But a nervous disorder which affected him prevented his sleeping well, and he invariably rose in the morning in the most unamiable of tempers. . . . He was so morbid about being stared at, that he would dismiss the very female servants of his own establishment if they were detected in the act of looking at him, utterly setting aside the time-worn axiom that a 'kitten may look at a king.'" On the other hand, Sir Benjamin Brodie, who attended him after his final return to the Castle, speaks more favourably :—"I generally went," he says, "to the King's apartments about ten in the morning, and sat by his bedside for one or two hours before my departure, during which he conversed on various subjects, not unfrequently speculating on his own condition and prospects. In his more sanguine moments, his mind would revert to the cottage which he had built at Windsor Park, and he expressed the pleasure which it would afford him to return to this his favourite retreat, as if he had found the comparatively retired life which he had led there much more suited to his taste than the splendour of Windsor Castle. The impression made on my mind by the very limited observation which I was able to make on these occasions was, that the King would have been a happier and a better man if it had been his lot to be nothing more than a simple country gentleman, instead of being in the exalted position which he inherited."

"I was at the Royal Lodge for one night last Wednesday," writes Mr. Greville, in June, 1827; "about thirty people sat down to dinner, and the company was changed nearly every day. It is a delightful place to live in, but the rooms are too low, and too small for very large parties. Nothing can exceed the luxury of the internal arrangements. The King was very well, and in excellent spirits, but very weak in his knees, and could not walk without difficulty. The evening passed off tolerably, owing to the Tyrolese, whom Esterhazy (the Austrian ambassador) brought down to amuse the King, and he was so pleased with them that he made them sing and dance before him the whole evening; the women kissed his face, and the men his hand, and he talked to them in German. Though this evening went off well enough, it is clear that nothing would be more insupportable than to live at this court; the dulness must be excessive, and the people who compose his habitual society are the most insipid and uninteresting that can be found. As for Lady Conyngham, she looks bored to death, and she never speaks, never appears to have one word to say to the King, who, however, talks himself without ceasing."

Nearly two years later, Mr. Greville sketches what he calls "the King's most extraordinary life." He never rose, it appears, "till six in the afternoon." His attendants roused him, and opened the window curtains at six or seven o'clock in the morning; but he breakfasted in bed, did whatever business he could be prevailed upon to do in bed also, read every newspaper diligently from the first line to the last, dozed three or four hours, got up in time for dinner, and retired to bed between ten and eleven. "He sleeps very ill," adds this cynical chronicler of small beer, "and rings his bell forty times in the night; if he wants to know the hour, though a watch hangs close to him, he will have his *valet de chambre* down rather than turn his head to look at it. The same thing if he wants a glass of water; he won't stretch out his hand to get it. His valets are nearly destroyed, and at last Lady Conyngham prevailed on him to agree to an arrangement by which they wait on him on alternate days. The service is still most severe, as on the days they are in waiting their labours are incessant, and they cannot take off their clothes at night, and hardly lie down. He is in good health, but irritable." We need quote no further. It is earnestly to be hoped that no future English King will lead so useless and poor a life as George IV. led; or, at least, if such be the case, that no such bitterly faithful historian as Mr. Greville will register its paltry details!

During the earlier and happier years of the present reign, considerable improvements were effected at Windsor, under the direction of Mr. Salvin, and at the suggestion of the Prince Consort. Everywhere may now be seen the impress of high culture and a refined taste. The Lower Ward has been carefully and accurately restored in a strictly mediæval spirit; St. George's Chapel has been invested with novel splendour; and, more recently, the Wolsey Chapel, or Tomb-House, has been converted into a costly memorial of "the Good Prince."

Some glimpses of life at Windsor, while the Prince was still by the Queen's side, may be obtained from the pages of the "Memoir of Baron Bunsen," for several years Prussian Minister and Envoy Extraordinary at the British Court. Thus he writes, under the date of September 25th, 1846 :—" I arrived here yesterday at six, and at eight o'clock all followed the Queen in to dinner in the great hall hung round with Waterloo portraits. The band, so placed as to be invisible, played exquisitely, so that what with the fine proportions of the hall, and the well-subdued light, and the splendour of the plate and decorations, the scene

THE WATERLOO CHAMBER.

was such as fairy tales present; and Lady Canning, Miss Dawson, and Miss Stanley were beautiful enough to personate the ideal attendants of an ideal court. The Queen looked well and *rayonnante*, with that expression which she always has when thoroughly pleased with all that occupies her mind, which, you know, I always observe with delight, as fraught with that truth and reality which so essentially belong to her character, and so strongly distinguish her countenance, in all its changes, from the *fixed mask* only too common in the royal ranks of society.

"We all spoke German, and the Princess Royal, by desire of the Queen, read a fable out of one of the books perfectly well. The Queen often spoke with me about education, and, in particular, of religious instruction. Her views are very serious, but at the same time liberal and comprehensive. She (as well as Prince Albert) hates all formalism. The Queen reads a good deal.

" . . . In the morning, I accompanied the royal party to the terrace to see the troops, who fired a *feu de joie* in honour of the Prince of Wales, who enjoyed it much, in extreme seriousness, and returned duly, by a military salute, the salutation he received as the colours passed. . . . It was with a solemn consciousness that I paced up and down, before breakfast, in the fine corridor, and beheld the sunshine with the clearest blue sky above the towers and turrets ; meditating upon the happiness that dwells within those walls, founded on reason, integrity, and love—a pattern of the well-ordered and inwardly vigorous and flourishing life that spreads all around, even to the extremities of the great island. . . . I should best have liked to have had your children with us to see what I saw that evening between five and six o'clock, when we were allowed to follow the Queen and Prince Albert a long way, through one large room after another, till we came to one where hung a red curtain, which was presently drawn aside for a representation of the Four Seasons, studied and contrived by the royal children as a surprise to the Queen in celebration of her wedding-day. First appeared Princess Alice as the Spring, scattering flowers and reciting verses, which were taken from Thomson's 'Seasons.' She moved gracefully, and spoke in a distinct and pleasing manner, with excellent modulation, and a tone of voice sweet and penetrating, like that of the Queen. Then the curtain was drawn and the scene changed, and the Princess Royal represented Summer, with Prince Arthur stretched upon the sheaves, as if tired with the heat and harvest-work. Another change, and Prince Alfred, with a cover of vine-leaves and the skin of a panther, represented Autumn, looking very well. Then followed a change to a winter landscape, and the Prince of Wales represented Winter, with a cloak covered with icicles (or what seemed such), and the Princess Louise, a charming little muffled-up figure, busy keeping up a fire, the Prince reciting (as all had done) passages, more or less modified, from Thomson. Then followed the last change, when all the Seasons were grouped together, and far behind, on a height, appeared Princess Helena, with a long white veil hanging on both sides down to her feet, holding a long cross, and pronouncing a blessing on the Queen and the Prince. The Princess Helena looked very charming. This was the close ; but, by command of the Queen, the curtain was again withdrawn, and we saw the whole royal family together, who came down from their raised platform ; also the baby, Prince Leopold, was carried in by his nurse, and looked at us all with big eyes, stretching out his arms to be taken by the Prince Consort."

It is unnecessary to dwell further on the happy wedded life of the Queen ; on the perfect sympathy which existed between her and her admirable husband; on the consummate pattern of domestic bliss which was so long set up before the eyes of a loyal people. Even the fierce light which beats upon a throne has revealed nothing mean or ungraceful in the character or career of the late Prince Consort, and his premature death must always be one of the saddest and tenderest of the associations of Windsor Castle.

In conclusion, we may glance briefly at the ballad-history of Windsor. In the earlier

"Songs of the People" it figures largely. Thus, in the lively satire which, in the reign of Henry III., was directed against the sayings and doings of Richard, the King of the Romans, we read :—

> "By God, that is above us, he did much sin
> That let passin over sea the Earl of Warraine ;
> He hath robbed England, the moors, and the fens,
> The gold and the silver, and carried them hence.
> For love of Windesore,
> Richard, tho' thou be ever trichard,
> Trichen shalt thou never more."

Into his "Romaunt of the Rose" Chaucer introduces Edward III., the "Lord of Windsor," and his son, the great popular hero, Edward the Black Prince. The famous story of King Edward and his passion for the beautiful Countess of Salisbury, told so graphically by Froissart, is associated with Windsor by a contemporary balladist, who seems to have possessed a true dramatic instinct, and manages the conclusion of the romance with much effectiveness. Terse are the speeches exchanged between the virtuous beauty and her royal suitor :—

> "And I consent, if you will grant one boon to me."
> "I grant it, lady fair, whate'er it be."
> "My husband is alive, you know—
> First, let me kill him, ere I go,
> And at your command for ever will I be."
> "Thy husband now in France doth rest."
> "No, no ! he lies within my breast,
> And being so nigh, he will my falsehood see."

Uncovering her snowy bosom, the Countess raises her hand to deal the blow which will save her from dishonour. Edward, conscience-stricken, seizes her hand, snatches the uplifted dagger, and swears by his kingly word never to offend her ears again.

In the ballad of "The Poor Man and the King," the former, who figures as chief character, follows the King to his royal castle, and, telling the simple story of his wrongs, obtains redress :—

> "He hath gotten a grey russet gown on his back,
> And a hood well buckled under his chin,
> And a large staff upon his neck,
> And he is to Windsor to our King.
>
> "So when he came to Windsor Hall,
> The gates were shut as he there stood ;
> He knocked and poked with a great long staff,
> The porter had thought he had been wood.
>
> "He knocked again with might and main ;
> Said, 'You, ho! Is our King within ?'
> With that he proffered a great reward—
> A single penny to let him come in."

The ballad of "King Edward and the Shepherd," of which Mr. Hepworth Dixon furnishes a pleasant epitome, is one of a kind that has always been popular in all countries, and may be traced in its origin to the lands of the East. Edward, when out a-riding on a sweet morning of May, meets with a simple shepherd, who does not recognise his person, and enters freely into talk with him :—

> "The King to the herd said then,
>   'Of whence art thou, good man?'
>   'In Windsor was I born,
>   It is a mile but here before ;
>   I am so filled with the King
>   That I must fly from my woning,
>   And therefore woe is me !
>   I had my cattle, now I have none.'"

The King is shocked to hear of the wrong-doing of his officers, and invites the shepherd to come next day to Windsor Castle, and pour his complaint into the royal ear, hinting that he has a friend at court who will introduce him even into the Presence. The shepherd informs him that five pounds two shillings are owing to him from the King's men, but that he has no other proof than a bit of hazel twig. "What is thy name?" says the King. "Adam the shepherd; and what is thine?" "Jolly Robin." So the two grew great friends, Adam promising to visit the Castle, and vowing that if Robin procure him his five pounds two shillings, he shall have seven bright shillings for himself. Robin remarks that he is hungry, and straightway Adam invites him to take a bite and sup in his cottage ; an invitation which is eagerly accepted. There the shepherd's wife spreads a cloth upon the table, and produces white bread and sparkling twopenny ale, accompanied by such truly royal dishes as a heron, a crane, and a wild swan. They dine and drink, and cap each other's merry jests. Edward soon discovers that his shepherd is not the simple swain he supposed, and, to test him, lets fall a remark that he is hugely fond of a slice of good venison. "Canst thou keep a secret?" inquires Adam, with a laugh in his eye. When assured of his guest's discretion, he accumulates hart pie, coney pie, roe pie upon the board. "All alive yesterday," he chuckles, "and came into the house by moonlight." Next, as *arbiter bibendi*, he teaches his new friend the right fashion of drinking. "Passylodion!" he cries, as he lifts his cup; and "Berafryord!" rejoins Robin, according to instruction; "Passylodion" meaning "To your health!" and "Berafryord" "Heel-taps, and fill again!"

> "Thus they sate withouten ship,
>   The King with Adam and his wife,
>   And made him merry and glad ;
>   The shepherd bade the cup fill,
>   The Kinge to drinke had good will,
>   His wife did as he bade.
>   When the cup was come anon,
>   The King said ' Passylodion !'"

Next day Adam arrives at the Castle, and is admitted by the porter, who has received his orders from the King. With Edward are his cousin of Lancaster and the Earls of Stafford and Warren, all three of course being in the secret. "I'll wager, now," says Edward, with a laugh—"I'll wager a tun of wine, that though the best lord among you shall hail to this rustic, he will not return the courtesy by doffing his cap." Stafford steps forward. "Hail, good man! whither wilt thou go?" Without removing his bonnet, Adam answers that he wants to see Jolly Robin. The mystification is carried on for some time longer, but at last Adam is made to understand that Jolly Robin and King Edward are one and the same person. Judge of his surprise and alarm when he bethinks himself of the frank confidences of the previous evening; of the venison that came home by moonlight, and cost never a penny; of the hart pie, and roe pie, and coney pie; of the cups of foaming ale, and the toasts of "Berafryord" and "Passylodion." The King, however, hastens to reassure him; entertains him with truly royal hospitality, and sends him away a happier and richer man than he came.

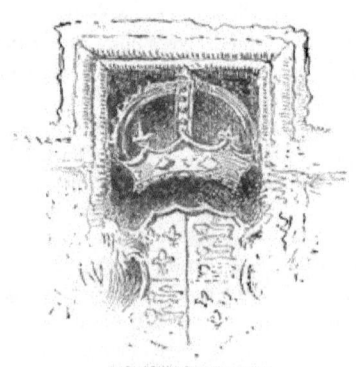

(OLD SCULPTURED ARMS.)

ST GEORGES CHAPEL

CHAPTER XI.

WINDSOR CASTLE AS IT IS.

TO George IV. is due the present stately aspect of the Castle. Successive additions had rendered it as abnormal in outward appearance as it was defective in internal convenience; so that it needed a wholesale restoration and reconstruction. The architect employed was Mr. Jeffry Wyatt, afterwards knighted as Sir Jeffry Wyattville; and the necessary funds were liberally voted by Parliament. The eastern section of the building was entirely reconstructed, at an outlay of upwards of £1,000,000; and though it is easy to detect irregularities and to point out examples of bad taste, the general effect is so soberly magnificent, and carries with it such an air of grave dignity, that the architect may well receive our commendation. He continued to superintend the works until his death in 1840. His task was then taken up by other hands, under the general oversight of the late Prince Consort, who restored the Lower Ward from the designs of Mr. Salvin. St. George's Chapel has likewise been renewed; the Entrance Hall and State Staircase have been rebuilt, and the Royal Apartments remodelled and re-embellished—on the whole, with a fine taste and an accuracy of detail that have left little to be desired.

The Castle buildings now extend about 1500 feet from east to west, with a breadth of from 400 to 500 feet; covering a ridge of high land which, at its western extremity, sinks down to the Thames. They are divided into three Wards or Courts: the Upper, which contains the Royal Apartments, occupying the eastern portion; the Middle, centering round the grandiose pile of the Round Tower; and the Lower, which includes St. George's Chapel, the Deanery, and the Cloisters, forming the western portion.

To the Lower Ward, which is necessarily the most ancient, our attention must first be directed. We approach it from the town by King Henry VIII.'s Gateway; and observe that it is protected by a massive wall and several towers, of which the Clewer (also called the Bell or Cæsar) Tower and the Garter Tower (restored by Mr. Salvin) belong to the reign of Henry III. The Wykeham, or Winchester Tower, was built for Edward III. by William of Wykeham, afterwards Bishop of Winchester. It flanks the North Terrace on the west. Of later date are the Salisbury Tower, the official residence of the Chancellor of the Order of the Garter, and the Wardrobe Tower. The only portions belonging to the Norman Castle are the doorways at each end of a subterranean passage cut through the chalk, so as to open into the outer fosse.

The present College Library was the royal Hall of that splendid "Domus Regis" of Henry III., which Matthew of Westminster declared to be the most magnificent royal dwelling in Europe. Of its Royal Kitchen and King's Chamber only scanty traces are extant; but the Galilee Porch of the Memorial Chapel, and the south ambulatory of the Dean's Cloister, retain their ancient character.

THE WINCHESTER TOWER.

St. George's Chapel was begun by Edward IV. on the site of an earlier foundation rebuilt by Henry III. Its style of architecture is the Perpendicular, of which there are few finer specimens in England. Richard Beauchamp, Bishop of Salisbury, was first appointed to superintend its erection; to him succeeded Sir Reginald Bray, the confidential adviser of Henry VII.; but the entire design was not completed until the reign of Henry VIII.

The ground-plan is cruciform; but the transepts are of such small proportions, that they might fitly be designated octagonal bays. On entering the interior, we are impressed by the splendour of the general effect, which almost precludes us from duly observing the beauty and harmony of the several details. The panelled walls, the shapely columns with their rich fern-like tracery, the high groined roof, the emblazoned windows, the dark oaken stalls in the Choir, over which hang suspended the banners, helms, and mantles of the knights of the famous Order of the Garter—that Order which "exceeds," as Selden says, "in majesty, honour, and fame, all chivalrous orders in the world, and has precedence of antiquity before the eldest rank of honour of that kind anywhere established"—all this pomp and circumstance make a powerful appeal to the imagination. At the back of each stall is a brass plate, bearing the name of its knightly occupant. The royal stall, on the right, is distinguished by a large banner of velvet, mantled with silk.

The roof of the Choir will repay "an upward glance." It was designed by Sir Reginald Bray in 1508, and the cost of its construction defrayed by the then Knights of the Garter. Among the devices "carven in stone" which enrich it, may be seen the armorial bearings of Edward the Confessor, Edward III., the Black Prince, Henry VI., Henry VII., and Henry VIII., the arms of England and France quartered, the Holy Cross, the Rose, the Portcullis, and St. George's shield, while fantastic heraldic emblazoning surrounds and connects the scutcheons of many of the oldest and noblest English houses.

On a stone in the centre of the Choir may be read the names of the illustrious personages interred in the vault beneath—Henry VIII., Jane Seymour, Charles I. The coffin of the last-named was opened on the

THE NORMAN GATE.

1st of April, 1813, in the presence of the Prince Regent, the Duke of Cumberland, the Dean of Windsor, and others, and an examination of the remains made by Sir Henry Halford. The body was found in tolerable preservation, amidst the gums and resins which coated it. The complexion of the face was dark and discoloured. The forehead and temples had lost little or nothing of their muscular substance; the cartilage of the nose was gone; but the left eye, in the first moment of exposure, was open and full, though it vanished almost immediately; and the pointed beard, so characteristic of the reign of King Charles, was perfect. The shape of the face was a long oval. On examination, the head was found to be loose, and was easily taken up and held to view. The hair was thick at the back, and, in appearance, nearly black. On holding up the head to examine the place of separation from the body, the muscles of the neck had evidently retracted themselves considerably, and the fourth cervical vertebra was found to be cut through its substance transversely, leaving the surfaces of the divided portions perfectly smooth and even.

Nearer the Altar is the entrance to the vault which contains the dust of George III., George IV., William IV., Queens Charlotte and Adelaide, the Dukes of Kent and York, the Princesses Amelia, Augusta, and Charlotte, and the late King George of Hanover.

The east window, restored a few years ago, from the designs of Sir G. G. Scott, comprises four tiers of lights, and forms a remarkable "In Memoriam" of the late Prince Consort. It is filled with painted glass by Clayton and Bell. The lowest tier exhibits, in fourteen pictures, various aspects of the Prince's admirable and useful life. In the next tier, the central subject, represented in seven lights, is the Adoration of the Magi, flanked on the one hand by the Kings of Judah—Asa, Jehoshaphat, Hezekiah, Josiah; on the other by New Testament saints—Nicodemus, Gamaliel, the Good Centurion, and Timothy. Seven lights in the third tier are devoted to the Resurrection, with four lights, on the one side, exhibiting Abraham, Joseph, Samuel, Daniel, and on the other, John, James, Bartholomew, and Barnabas. Above all shines the Glory of the Saviour, with angels and archangels depositing their crowns before His throne. The Latin inscription is to the effect that the Dean and Canons of Windsor have dedicated this window "to the honour of God and the memory of the deeply-regretted Prince." The rich alabaster Reredos, with its sculptures of our Lord's appearance to the disciples (after His resurrection), and the Ascension, forms a part of this memorial.

The west window, containing sixteen lights in five tiers, is filled with gorgeously-coloured figures of prophets, saints, kings, and knights, while the upper portion is emblazoned with royal badges.

To the west of the Altar is the Royal Closet, or Queen's Gallery, now used by the Sovereign when she attends Divine service, but originally intended for such favoured individuals as were allowed to witness the splendid ceremonial of the installation of Knights of the Garter. It will be remembered that from this closet the Queen, dressed in deepest mourning, witnessed the marriage of the Prince of Wales to Alexandra of Denmark. Underneath it stands the defaced tomb of Edward IV. Its rich iron screen, formerly attributed to Antwerp's artist-smith, Quentin Matsys, is now generally supposed to have been the work of Edward IV.'s artificer, John Tresilan. On a slab within the tomb are engraved the names of "Edward IV. and his Queen, Elizabeth Wydville;" on the opposite choir are read those of Henry VI. and Sir Charles Brandon, Duke of Suffolk, whom Mary

Tudor, the strong-minded sister of Henry VIII., married for love, soon after the death of her first husband, Louis XII. of France (1515).

Of the splendid scenes and pageants of chivalry which St. George's Chapel has so often witnessed, we may form an idea by reference to the pages of the old chroniclers.* We take from the pages of Stow the following account of a Garter festival in the sixteenth year of the reign of Edward IV. :—

Towards the time of even-song, the King, with the Knights of the Order, all clothed in blue, and mounted on horseback, rode to the Chapter-house, and thence marched on foot to the Choir, where they remained till even-song was over; after which they returned to the Castle, mounted and apparelled as before, and had their "void of spices" and other refreshments.

On Sunday morning, King and Knights rode to matins, which being ended, they entered the Chapter, and thence repaired to the Dean's house to breakfast, and after to the Choir again, every Knight to his own stall. Then came the Queen, with the Lady Elizabeth, her eldest daughter (afterwards wife to Henry VII.), the Duchess of Suffolk, the King's sister, the Marchioness of Montague, the Marchioness of Dorset, the Lady Hastings, and other beauties and dames of her brilliant Court, all attired in the same "livery of murrey," embroidered with garters," except her ladyship of Montague, who rode in a gown of silk. These *belles dames* were placed in the rood loft, the whole spectacle realising the poet's vision of

THE QUEEN'S CLOSET.

> "Things of Knights and barons bold,
> In weeds of peace, . . .
> With store of ladies, whose bright eyes
> Rain influence."

In the same order and habit came the Sovereign and Knights, with the Queen and her ladies, in the afternoon to even-song. That day King Edward dined in his great chamber, with Beauchamp, Bishop of Salisbury, Chancellor of the Order, on his right, and

---

* Among memorable scenes which this chapel has witnessed may be mentioned the marriage of the Black Prince with the fair Joan of Kent, and, in our own times, those of the Prince of Wales with the Princess Alexandra, and the Duke of Connaught with the Princess Louisa Margaret; also the installation of Napoleon III. as a Knight of the Garter.

on his left his brother and brother-in-law, the Duke of Clarence and the Duke of Suffolk. At a side table sat the Marquis of Dorset, one of the most accomplished nobles of the age; the Earls of Arundel, Northumberland, and Essex; the Lord Maltravers, the Earl Douglas; the Lords Dudley, Ferrars, and Howard, and Sir John Astley. And at an opposite table sat Master Dudley, Dean of St. George's Chapel, along with the Canons of the same Chapel, in their mantles of murrey and roundlet of St. George.

On the Monday, the Sovereign and Knights of the Order entered the Chapter, where they had a short communication, whence they went to the Choir, where every Knight stood before his stall, while the King offered at the altar a rich suit of vestments and certain copes of the same suit, which the Dean received. That done, the King retired to his stall, and each Knight sat him down in his own stall, till the offertory. And then the Marquis of Dorset and the Duke of Suffolk offered the sword of John Mowbray, late Duke of Norfolk, deceased; the Lord Maltravers and Howard, his baton; which being done, and obeisance made, every Knight stood before his stall, while the King offered, and then every Knight offered according to his stall—to wit, the Duke of Clarence, the Marquis of Dorset, the Duke of York, the Earl of Arundel, the Earl of Essex, the Duke of Suffolk, the Earl of Northumberland, the Earl Douglas, the Lord Maltravers and the Lord Howard the Lord Dudley, the Lord Ferrars, and Sir John Astley.

Henry VIII. resembled Edward IV. in many points of character, but in none more closely than in his love of pomp and pageantry. He raised the Order of the Garter to the rank of an European institution, enrolling among its members Charles V. of Germany, Ferdinand, King of the Romans, and Francis I. of France, and he celebrated its festivals with unparalleled magnificence. Let us glance at that which was held here on the 28th of May, 1523, and which has been described by the antiquary, Elias Ashworth:—

"On the previous day, being Friday, the King removed from Richmond towards his Castle of Windsor, and appointed the hour of one in the afternoon for all noblemen and others who should wait upon his Grace to be ready to attend him between Richmond and Hounslow. And because of a scarcity and straitness of lodgings, as well as in avoidance and eschewing of the corrupt air, every nobleman was taxed and rated to a certain number of horse—that is to say, every Duke at 60 horses, Marquis at 50 horses, every Earl at 40 horses, every Baron at 30 horses, every Knight of the Garter, bachelor, at 20 horses, and no other Knight or nobleman to have above 16 horses, with their carriages and all. And thus right nobly accompanied, the King rode to Colnbrook, and at the sign of the Katherine's Wheel the King took his courser, and his henchmen, richly apparelled, followed, and also the King's horse of state, led : Garter King of Arms wore his coat-of-arms; the Lord Richard Fox, Bishop of Winchester and Prelate of the Order, with many other 'grave estates,' gave their attendance upon his Highness. The Queen—[this was Katherine of Arragon—

'That, like a jewel, had hung
About his neck, yet never lost her lustre;
Of her who loves him with that excellence
That angels love good men with; even of her
That, when the greatest stroke of fortune falls,
Will bless the King']—

the Queen and her ladies, and their companies, stood in the field at the town's end beside the highway towards Windsor, to see the King's noble procession ride by, with blare of music and amid the acclamations of the multitude; and afterwards rode to the ferry, and proceeded towards the Castle. The King rode onward slowly to Eton College, where all they of the College stood 'in manner of procession' to receive his Grace, after their custom.

"The King entered Windsor with his great horses—that is to say, nine horses with nine Children of Honour upon them, and the Master of the King's horses upon another great courser's back following them, having and leading the King's horse of estate in his hand—that is to say, a rich courser with a rich saddle, and trapped and garnished, following the King—and so entered the Castle.

"At the Castle-gate, the Ministers of the College received the King in procession; and the King and Knights of the Order, at the Church-door, took their mantles, and entered the Choir. All the Knights stood there before their stalls until the Sovereign had offered, and returned to *his* stall; after which every Knight made his offering as by statute ordained, and took his seat; a long ceremony, because of the great number of Knights present, nineteen in all, besides the Sovereign. In attendance on the King were all his high officers and heralds, glittering in their coats-of-arms; and all his trumpets, who filled the Chapel with silver sounds while the King made his entry. The Lord Montague bore the sword of state before the King, and Garter King of Arms rode next before the sword, with Sir William Compton on his left hand, carrying the Black Rod."

It may be noted that gossiping Pepys visited St. George's Chapel in the reign of Charles II., and has left the following record of the visit:—" We took coach to Windsor to the Garter, and thither sent for Dr. Childs, who came to us, and carried us to St. George's Chapel, and there placed us among the stalls of the Knights (and pretty the observation, that no man, but a woman, may sit in a Knight's place, where any brass plates are set); and hither came cushions to us, and a young singing-boy to bring us a copy of the Anthem to be sung. And here, for our sakes, had this Anthem and the great service sung extraordinary, only to entertain us. It is a noble place indeed, and a good choir of voices. Great bowing by all the people, the Poor Knights particularly, to the altar. After prayers we went to see the plate of the Chapel and the robes of Knights, and a man to show us the banners of the several Knights in being which hang over the stalls. And so to other discourse very pretty, about the Order. Was shown where the late King Charles was buried, and King Henry the Eighth and my Lady Seymour."

Let us now pay a rapid visit to the various chapels.

The Bray Chapel occupies the south transept. Its founder, Sir Reginald Bray, was interred here in 1502. A black marble slab indicates the resting-place of the learned defender of the Athanasian Creed, Dr. Waterland. There are also memorials to several bishops (including one in alabaster to Dr. Giles Thompson, Bishop of Gloucester), to Lord Langford (died 1825), and Henry Carlyon, the architect (died 1815).

The west transept forms the Rutland Chapel, and was built by Sir Thomas St. Leger as a mausoleum for his wife, Anne, Duchess of Exeter, sister of Edward IV.—a lady who figures in "the Paston Letters." A brass represents husband and wife kneeling before a crucifix. There is also a brass for Robert Honeywood, Canon of Windsor, died 1522. Sir Thomas St. Leger's daughter, Anne, and her husband, Lord Ros, an ancestor of the noble family of Manners (died 1513), are commemorated by a stately monument, adorned with their recumbent effigies. Here, too, lie buried the Duchess of St. Albans (died 1741); Major Pack, killed at Waterloo; and Dr. Aylward, the musician.

The Lincoln Chapel contains the superb altar-tomb of Edward Earl of Lincoln, Lord High Admiral, died 1584, who, both as soldier and statesman, deserved and attained distinction. It is constructed of alabaster, with shafts of porphyry, and embellished with recumbent marble effigies of the Earl and his widow (who erected the monument), as well as with figures in relief of their five sons and three daughters. Here also lies the dust of the once illustrious Richard Beauchamp, Bishop of Salisbury, first Chancellor of the Order of the Garter. The bones of "Maister John Schorn, that blesséd man born," were brought hither by Bishop Beauchamp from North Marston, in Buckinghamshire. This remarkable person, though never canonised, attained all the honours of sanctity, and cast an odour about his tomb which prevailed until after the Reformation. It was thought that he had the power of curing the ague—a disease more general in the days before sanitary reform than at present, and very widely dreaded. It was also a matter of belief that he once conjured the devil into a boot; and an ancient screen, still existing in Gately Church, Norfolk, represents him holding a boot in his left hand, with the devil peeping out of it. A well near North Marston Church, known as Master John Shorne's Well, was credited with the possession of healing powers by those who drank of its waters. So great was his reputation, that the presents offered at his shrine were estimated to amount to a yearly value of £300, or about £3600 of our current money. A ballad of the Reformation period ridicules his pretensions and his votaries:—

> " To Maister John Schorn, that blesséd man born,
> For the ague to him we apply,
> Which judgeth with a bote, I beshrew his heart rote
> That will trust him, and it be I."

Observe the black-letter Bible, in a recess opposite the tomb, which has been substituted for the Breviary formerly placed here by Bishop Beauchamp, as an assistance

ROUND TOWER WINDSOR

to "priests and ministers of God's Church saying thence their divine service, and for all other that listen to say thereby their devotion."

The Oxenbridge Chapel, founded in 1522 by a canon of that name, is dedicated to St. John Baptist, three events in whose history are figured in a remarkable triptych.

These two chapels are on the south. Opposite to them are the Hastings and the Aldworth. The Hastings Chapel was built by Elizabeth, wife of William Lord Hastings, the debonnair chamberlain of Edward IV., afterwards beheaded, on a charge of high treason, by order of Richard III. It is dedicated to St. Stephen, and separated from the choir by an open screen of elegant design. The roof is groined; the walls are ornamented with statues of saints and angels, displaying the armorial bearings of the Hastings family. Four mural paintings illustrate leading incidents in the career of St. Stephen—his preaching to the Jews, his appearance before the tribunal, his martyrdom, and his beatification. The Aldworth Chapel was founded by Bishop Oliver King in 1492. It contains the Bishop's altar-tomb of grey marble, and the graves of the family of Aldworth. Near this chapel is placed the tomb, in white marble and serpentine, erected by Queen Victoria as "a tribute of respect and affection" to Mary, Duchess of Gloucester, died 1859. It was designed by Sir G. G. Scott. The bas-reliefs, in white marble, by Theed, are descriptive of the charitable acts of "clothing the naked," "feeding the hungry," "relieving the wanderer," and "ministering to the sick."

The Beaufort Chapel, dedicated to the Virgin Mary, was founded by Charles Somerset, Earl of Worcester (died 1526); but his tomb, and that of Henry, first Duke of Beaufort (died 1699), were removed, in 1874, to take their place among the Beaufort memorials in Badminton Church, and the chapel was converted into a mausoleum for Edward, Duke of Kent. His sarcophagus, designed by Sir G. G. Scott, is of alabaster and coloured marbles; the recumbent effigy was executed by Mr. Boehm.

The Urswick Chapel contains the ill-conceived but gorgeously-wrought cenotaph, by M. C. Wyatt, of the Princess Charlotte, whose premature death, in 1817, awakened such an outburst of passionate regret throughout the kingdom. The coloured windows in the rear are decorated with figures of six of the Apostles, and the lights are so arranged as to throw, when the sun shines, a golden glory on the marble tomb. Close by is the monument to the Princess's husband, Leopold, King of the Belgians, erected by the Queen. The recumbent effigy, in white marble, was the work of Miss Durant.

Almost opposite the Chapter-room may be seen Sevier's fine marble monument to Field-Marshal the Earl of Harcourt, in his peer's robes; and in the same aisle is situated the monument of the distinguished soldier Lieutenant General Sir John Elley, K.C.B., who died in 1839. Sir John Elley, who rose from the ranks, served with high honour in the Peninsular campaigns of Wellington.

To the east of St. George's Chapel is situated the Albert Memorial Chapel, formerly known as the Tomb-house, or Wolsey Chapel. Originally founded by Henry VII., Wolsey obtained a grant of it from the Crown, completed it, and began to build within it a sumptuous altar-tomb for himself or his royal master. His fall prevented the accomplishment of his design. During the sway of the Long Parliament, the chapel was dismantled, and the figures on the tomb were sold as metal.* The black marble sarcophagus escaped destruction, but no use was made of it until 1805, when it was selected for the tomb of Nelson. George III. caused a crypt to be constructed beneath the chapel as a vault for the royal family, and the chapel then received the name of the Tombhouse. The entrance to the vault, however, was opened up in St. George's Chapel; and the Tomb-house remained without object or utility until appropriated by the Queen as a memorial to the Prince Consort. For this purpose the architectural work was entrusted to Sir G. G. Scott, and the decorative to Baron Triqueti; and for ten years was liberally supplied

ALBERT MEMORIAL CHAPEL.

the annual sum required to defray the heavy cost. The result of all this labour and devotion is a splendid spectacle; open to criticism, perhaps, in some of its details, but, undoubtedly, very effective and impressive as a whole, and based, in the design, upon certain well-understood and harmonious principles. As in the case of the Royal Mausoleum, all the available space in the interior is covered with decorative work, sculpture, or mosaic, costly in material and elaborate in execution. The floor is a mosaic of coloured marbles. The golden groined roof is filled in with emblematical mosaics, executed by Signor Salviati from Clayton and Bell's designs. The chancel windows glow with rich painted

* The chapel was fitted up by James II. for the Roman worship, much to the indignation of the "Protestant mob," who broke the windows and destroyed the decorations. In George II.'s reign it was occupied by the Free Grammar School.

glass by Clayton and Bell. The four-light windows in the apse, by the same artists, illustrate the Garden of Eden, the Garden of Gethsemane, the Garden of St. Joseph, the Garden of the Blessed, and the Passion. The windows in the nave supply a commentary on the ancestral history of the Prince Consort, and the mosaics in the west window are a portrait-gallery of kings and nobles connected with Windsor Castle. The interspaces between the windows are filled with picture-tablets, by Baron Triqueti—formed by inlaying, somewhat after the style of the tarsia work of mediæval Florence, marbles and spars of different colours, with coloured and dark cements, on a ground of white Sicilian marble. There are fifteen of these tablets, representing the Passion, Old Testament episodes, and the virtues of "the Good Prince." Each is surrounded by a mosaic framework, and surmounted by a medallion of the Prince or Princess of the Royal Family at whose cost it was executed. Thus—No. 1 (on the right), Daniel in the Lion's Den; medallion of Prince Leopold. 2. Moses with the Books of the Law; Princess Louise. 3. Abraham presenting his son to Sara, after the meditated sacrificial offering at Jehovah-Jireh; Duke of Edinburgh. 4. Joseph appointed lord over all Egypt; Princess Alice. 5. Jacob blessing his children; Princess Imperial of Prussia. 6. The Crucifixion. 7. Angel at the Sepulchre. 8. Taking down our Lord from the Cross. 9. Christ at Gethsemane. 10. "And all Judah and Jerusalem mourned for Josiah;" Prince of Wales. 11. Jehoshaphat "taught all the people;" Princess of Wales. 12. The kings of the earth bringing presents to Solomon. 13. David writing the Psalms; Duke of Connaught. 14. Nathanael under the fig-tree; Princess Beatrice. The medallions were executed by Miss Durant, who, as well as Baron Triqueti, died before the Mausoleum was completed. Similar tablets in the apse are devoted to "the Entombment."

The reredos, finely carved, is of coloured marbles, alabaster, and white marble; the altar of Levantine marble, crowned with a Greek cross of agates and malachites.

The central point of all this artistic magnificence is formed by the altar-tomb of the Prince, which bears his recumbent effigy, clothed in mediæval armour "from top to toe," and adorned with the Garter insignia. The slab on which the figure rests is upheld by angels; the lateral niches are filled with statues of the Virtues, those at the ends with statues of the Queen, praying, and of Science, weeping. But it is surely an anti-climax to learn, after taking in the impressions produced by so much accumulated evidence of a deep and enduring grief and affection, that the Prince is buried—not here, but in the Mausoleum at Frogmore. One asks oneself—What, then, is the meaning of this sumptuous Tomb-house?

Passing onward in a northerly direction, we come to the Dean's Cloisters, erected by Robert of Burnham for Edward III. The south wall, the only relic extant of the St. George's Chapel built by Henry III., invites attention by its portrait of that monarch, crowned, and looking "every inch a king," which is known to have been the work of the monk, William of Westminster, in 1248. The tablets in these cloisters record the names of some of the Military Knights of Windsor (Edward III.'s *Milites Pauperes*), eighteen of whom are supported on the royal establishment, and lodged within the Castle walls. Of late years the knights have been carefully chosen from "gentlemen brought to necessity through adverse fortune, and such as have passed their lives in the service of their Prince." We may suppose that Mrs. Oliphant, in her recent novel, "Within the Precincts," which for the first time brings the knights upon the stage of fiction, depicts a state of things no longer in existence.

Dean Urswick built the Deanery in 1500; the façade exhibits his name and arms. In the rear of it rises the noble Winchester Tower, built by William of Wykeham, and for a while used by him as his residence. The inscription, *Hoc fecit Wykeham*, was cut by order of Sir Jeffry Wyattville.

THE DEAN'S CLOISTERS.

Leaving the visitor, if he be envious, to inspect the Canons' Cloister or the Hundred Steps (there are really one hundred and twenty-two), we betake ourselves to the Middle Ward, which, as we have already hinted, virtually consists of the Round Tower. This famous pile, formerly called " La Rose," was built by Edward III. to hold his " Table Round," which at first had been celebrated in the old Norman keep. " The pile was circular," says Dixon, " with an open gallery on the inner wall. Seated against the wall, and looking towards each other, two or three hundred knights could sit down to a common feast." Wykeham's Keep rose only fifty feet above the artificial mound, probably of British origin, on which it was planted. Sir Jeffry Wyattville, by a happy conception, raised it thirty feet higher, and added the Watch Tower, or Flag Turret, twenty-five feet, so that the topmost stone is 148 feet above the level of the quadrangle. By facing both the new part and the old with flints, he secured uniformity of appearance. When the sovereign is at Windsor, the Royal Standard, 36 feet by 27, floats from the majestic summit.

Among the illustrious prisoners of this Tower may be mentioned John, King of

France; David, King of Scotland; James I., King of Scotland; the Earl of Surrey; and the Marshal de Belleisle. The most distinguished of its governors was Prince Rupert, who filled the office after the Restoration.

The view which that summit commands is, we need hardly say, of wide extent. It embraces twelve counties; "tawny with corn and rye, bright with abundant pasture, and the red and white of kine and sheep, while here again the landscape is embrowned with groves and parks." The view is one of high interest, from the numerous scenes, celebrated in history or literature, or renowned for their loveliness, which it brings before the delighted vision. Looking upon them, we are fain to thank God that we live in such a land; a land where the Present is hallowed and enriched by the associations of the Past. Immediately beneath us, and separated only by the silver streak of the Thames, lies Eton, with its reminiscences of happy and auspicious boyhood. Further on lies Slough, where Sir William Herschel added a new planet to our solar system; Stoke Pogis, where in the classic and sacred shades sleeps the poet Gray; Upton, with its ivy-shrouded church-tower; Horton, with the blossomy garden where Milton meditated his rare poetic fancies; Beaconsfield, honoured by its memories of Waller the poet and Edmund Burke the statesman, and now made familiar to every tongue by the title of the astonishing scrivener's clerk who has boldly carved his way to the highest seat in the councils of the Queen; Binfield, where Pope

VIEW FROM ROUND TOWER, LOWER RAMPART.

"Lisped in numbers, and the numbers came;"

the picturesque village of Ivor, sleeping beside the "trouty Colne;" Burnham, with the leafy glory of its beeches; and Bulstrode, the noble seat of the Duke of Somerset. Note must also be taken of the undulating crests and green sides of St. Leonard's Hill, Priest's Hill, Cooper's Hill, St. Anne's Hill, and St. George's Hill.

The "Maiden's Tower" of the poet-Earl of Surrey was the ancient Rose Tower; an octagonal structure situated at the south-west angle of the Upper Ward, which derived its name from a carving of Edward IV.'s celebrated badge, the rose *en soleil*. On the bosses of the vaulted ceilings of the two lower chambers this decoration may still be seen; but the tower has otherwise lost all its original character, having been renovated and reconstructed by Sir Jeffry Wyattville.

Through William of Wykeham's Gateway, north of the Round Tower, we enter the Upper Ward, the site of Edward III.'s additions to the Castle. On the northern side are the State Apartments; on the eastern, the Queen's Private Apartments (the Queen's domestic rooms, so to speak); and on the southern, the apartments of the officials. The State entrance, north; south, between the York and Lancaster Towers, George IV.'s Gateway opens upon the Long Walk. At the west end stands an equestrian statue of Charles II., executed by one Josias Ibach Stada, for Tobias Rustat (Evelyn's "Toby Rustate"), a page of the backstairs, who presented it to his sovereign. The pedestal rejoices in a luxuriance of exquisite carving by Grinling Gibbons.

The extension of the Upper Ward to the summit of the Castle ridge is said to have been suggested to Edward by King John of France, when a prisoner at Windsor after the battle of Poitiers. The incident is picturesquely told by Mr. Hepworth Dixon :—

"Edward was at Windsor parleying with the King of France and King of Scots about his new buildings, when a jest, dropped by one of his captives, led to a great enlargement of the royal house. St. George's Chapel and St. George's College, with lodgings for the knights and canons, were rising from the ground. These works were in the Lower Ward. All that remained of Beauclerc's house were the Devil's Tower, the Lesser Hall, the King's Chamber, the Queen's Cabinet, and some domestic offices. The Upper Ward lay open towards the east, covered only by a parapet and ditch. Jean le Bon, a man of excellent taste in building, criticised the site :—

"'Your Grace's castle had been better on the higher ground than where it stands : there would be more to see, and your turrets would be visible a long way off.'

"David agreed with Jean. Struck by their remark, Edward replied in banter that their highnesses were right, and, acting on their lesson, he would bring his castle to the hill. They smiled. Edward explained that he would so enlarge his buildings by new rooms and galleries as to reach the pleasanter site. That would cost much money. Yes; but the ransoms of his critics should defray the cost of these great works.

"At the ensuing festival of St. George, King Jean said merrily, 'I have never seen such shows and feastings without an after reckoning in gold and silver coin.'

"His reckoning, when presented, proved a heavy bill; six million nobles, of which six hundred thousand were to be paid down, and forty thousand every year, till the last noble was discharged. . . . Seven years after his capture at Poitiers, Jean le Bon died in exile, leaving his name and memory at Windsor Castle, in the lodgings which he had occupied in King John's Tower, and in the Upper Ward, which his remarks had caused to be inclosed and surrounded by the Third King's House."

Such is the story; but we find it difficult to believe that the advantages of the site had not been previously detected by the keen eyes of Edward and his architect.

The State Apartments are inspected in the following order :—

The Queen's Audience Chamber, the walls of which are hung with fine Gobelin tapestry, illustrative of the history of Queen Esther, while the ceiling is all a-glow with one of Verrio's amazing allegories; Catherine of Braganza, represented as Britannia, proceeding to the Temple of Virtue, attended by Ceres, Flora, Pomona, and a bevy of goddesses. The portraits (Mary Queen of Scots, by Janet, and Frederick and William, Princes of Orange, by Honthorst) should be noticed, if only for their beautifully carved frames by Grinling Gibbons.

The ceiling was painted by Verrio, and in 1680 he received in payment a sum of £200. Horace Walpole relates that while this florid artist was employed at Windsor he quarrelled with a Mrs. Marriott, then acting as housekeeper, and revenged himself by borrowing "her ugly face for one of the Furies." To please the Court party, he represented the Earl of Shaftesbury (Anthony Ashley Cooper) among the Demons of Fashion, distributing libels abroad.

THE "MAIDEN'S TOWER."

Janet's curious picture of Mary Queen of Scots is covered with inscriptions in Latin. Translated, they read as follows :—" Mary, Queen of Scotland, by right Princess and legitimate heiress of England and Ireland, mother of James King of Great Britain, tormented by the heresy of her people, overcome by rebellion, and relying on the promise of her relation, Queen Elizabeth, repaired to England for safety in the year 1568. She was perfidiously detained a prisoner for nineteen years, when the English Parliament, stimulated by religious animosity, by an inhuman sentence condemned her to death, and on the 18th of February, 1587, she was beheaded by the common executioner, in the 45th year of her age and of her reign.

"Her most gracious Majesty, the daughter, consort, and mother of kings, is, in the presence of the officers and ministers of Queen Elizabeth, struck by the act of the executioner, and, after barbarously wounding her by a first and second blow, at the third attempt he severs the head from the body.

"Thus the once powerful Queen of France and Scotland ascends the fatal scaffold; with a mind unconquered but devout, she spurns at tyranny and treachery, she upholds the Catholic faith; her past and present life openly and clearly proclaim her a daughter of the Roman Church."

The Vandyck Room is rich in the possession of twenty-two of the finest works of this admirable painter. They represent—Henri, Comte de Berg; Charles I. in his royal robes, with his Queen on the one hand and Prince Charles on the other; Mary, Duchess of Richmond* (daughter of the elder Villiers, Duke of Buckingham), as St. Agnes, with laurel and palm-branch; the poets (*dii minores!*) Thomas Carew and William Killigrew; Henrietta Maria; the famous beauty, Lady Venetia Digby, whom her husband, quaint Sir Kenelm, so chivalrously worshipped, and the poets so lavishly praised (as, for instance, Ben Jonson, in his *Euphemc*—

> "Draw first a cloud all save her neck,
> And, out of that, make day to break;
> Till like her face it do appear,
> And men may think all light rose there.
>
> "Then let the beams of that disperse
> The cloud, and show the universe;
> But at such distance, as the eye
> May rather yet adore, than spy);

George and Francis Villiers, the two sons of the Duke of Buckingham; Thomas, Prince of Carignan, in armour; Henrietta Maria, a profile; Beatrice de Cusance, Princess of Cantecroix; Charles I.'s children—the well-known composition, introducing Prince Charles, the Princesses Mary and Elizabeth (on the right), the Princess Anne (on the left), and Prince James, seated apart, on a stool; the head of Charles I., in front face, profile, and three-quarters, painted for the use of Bernini the sculptor; the handsome *intriguante*, Lucy, Countess of Carlisle, reputed to have been Pym's mistress; Sir Kenelm Digby; Prince Charles, the Duke of York, and the Princess Mary (date 1638); Mary, Countess of Dorset;

---

* A pleasant anecdote is told of this lady's childhood, which was spent in the family of Charles I. One day she climbed a tree in the royal garden, to gather some fruit. The King, seeing her among the branches, mistook her for a large bird, and sent Mr. Porter, a handsome young gentleman of the Court, to kill it. On approaching the tree with his gun, he discovered the young lady, who, on being informed of his instructions, laughed heartily, and said she would have a "merry game." She caused herself to be stowed in a large hamper, and conveyed to the King's apartment. Mr. Porter then informed Charles that he had taken the bird alive; for it was so beautiful that, if he had killed it, he could never have forgiven himself. His Majesty, all eagerness to see it, opened the hamper, and the young beauty, clasping her arms round his neck, furnished him with an agreeable surprise.

Charles I., in armour, and on horseback, attended by the Duc d'Epernon, Master of the Horse (this noble picture has been frequently engraved. A careful examination of the canvas shows that the King's head had at one time been removed, and afterwards carefully replaced ; and it is supposed that when Charles I.'s gallery of paintings was announced for sale, some enthusiastic royalist adopted that mode of preserving the royal portrait from destruction, and replaced it after the Restoration); and a Portrait, traditionally but dubiously described as that of Vandyck's friend, Jan Sudenick.

The ceiling in this room is adorned with gilded panellings, enclosing the rose, the shamrock, and the thistle ; the royal arms, the initials of George III., palm branches, and other devices.

The Queen's State Drawing-Room, which is sumptuously furnished, contains two Scriptural subjects and some large landscapes by Zuccarelli, and portraits of Henry, Duke of Gloucester, youngest son of Charles I.; George I., George II., and Frederick, Prince of Wales, and his son, George III. The ceiling is very handsome ; and the rich silk damask hangings display the armorial bearings of William IV. and his consort, Queen Adelaide.

In the State Ante-Room, the ceiling is covered with Verrio's florid design of a Banquet of the Olympian Deities ; while the carving shows some of Grinling Gibbons's finest carved work—fish, fowl, fruit, and flowers being represented with the most exquisite delicacy and truthfulness. Surely never before or since was wood so plastic !

The Grand Staircase and Vestibule, constructed by Mr. Salvin, have an unquestionably imposing character, while their decorations are as rich as they are in fine taste. In a deep recess on the first landing stands Sir F. Chantrey's colossal marble statue of George IV. The Vestibule, 47 feet long, 28 feet wide, and 45 feet high, contains Boehm's statue of the Queen, attended by her favourite collie, several suits of armour of the sixteenth century, and numerous military trophies.

The Waterloo Chamber, 98 feet long, 47 feet broad, and 45 feet high, is the scene of the State banquets occasionally given by the Sovereign, when the buffets groan with costly gold and silver plate of the most *recherché* character. The walls are hung with the portraits of the royal personages, soldiers, and statesmen who were most prominently concerned in the conduct of the great Napoleonic war. They are thirty in number, and were mostly painted by Sir Thomas Lawrence. Of very unequal merit as works of art, they possess an enduring interest as historic memorials, and each suggests a train of instructive reflection. The reader will, therefore, be not displeased at an enumeration of them :—Duc de Richelieu, French Diplomatist ; General Overoff, a veteran Russian commander; Duke of Cambridge ; Earl of Liverpool, Prime Minister from 1812 to 1827 ; William IV.—painted by Sir David Wilkie ; George III.—painted by Sir William Beechy ; George IV.; Marquis of Londonderry, better known as Lord Castlereagh, Foreign Secretary from 1809 to 1822 ; Duke of York, British Commander-in-Chief ; Baron Humboldt (Wilhelm von), brother of the great scientific philosopher, Persian Ambassador; the Right Hon. George Canning, Foreign Secretary from 1807 to 1809, Ambassador at Lisbon, 1814 ; Earl Bathurst, Colonial

Secretary from 1812 to 1828; Count Münster, Hanoverian Diplomatist; Cardinal Gonsalvi, the Papal Minister; Prince Hardenberg, Prussian Minister for Foreign Affairs; William III., King of Prussia; Francis I., Emperor of Austria; Alexander I., Czar of Russia; Count Nesselrode, Russian Minister and Diplomatist; Pope Pius VII.; Count Capo d'Istria (or Cabodistrias) Russian Minister and Secretary to Alexander I.; Prince Metternich, Austrian Prime Minister; General Lord Hill—painted by H. W. Pickersgill; Charles X., King of France; Prince Schwartzenberg, Austrian General and Ambassador; Archduke Karl of Austria; General Sir Thomas Picton, fell at Waterloo—by Sir M. A. Shee; Duc d'Angoulême; Duke of Brunswick, killed at Quatre Bras—his father fell at Jena—

> ("Within a window'd niche of that high hall
> Sate Brunswick's fated chieftain; he did hear
> That sound the first amidst the festival,
> And caught its tone with Death's prophetic ear;
> And when they smiled because he deemed it near,
> His heart more truly knew that peal too well
> Which stretched his father on a bloody bier,
> And roused the vengeance blood alone could quell;
> He rushed into the field, and, foremost fighting, fell."
> BYRON, *Childe Harold*);

Leopold I., King of the Belgians; General Sir James Kempt—by H. W. Pickersgill; Count Platoff, Hetman of the Cossacks; The Duke of Wellington; Prince von Blucher (old "Marshal Vorwaerts," as his soldiers called him); Count Alten, by Reichmann; Marquis of Anglesea, by Sir M. A. Shee; Lieut.-Gen. Count Czernitschoff; and William Frederick, Prince of Orange.

It must be admitted that some of these "personages" have but small right to the distinguished places they occupy; while not a few illustrious names are "conspicuous by their absence."

The Grand Ball-Room, or Presence Chamber, measuring 94 feet by 34, is fitted up and furnished, as might be supposed, in the costliest manner, the style adopted being that known as the Louis Quatorze. The Gobelin tapestry which embellishes the walls, and embodies the old myth of Jason in quest of the Golden Fleece, recently told in such melodious verse by Mr. William Morris, was a present from Charles X. of France to George IV. Two richly wrought granite vases, a gift from Frederick III. of Prussia to William IV.; and a superb vase of malachite, sent by the Czar Nicholas to the Queen, are among the ornaments of this splendid chamber.

St. George's Hall, used for State banquets and the Garter festivals, was designed by Sir Jeffry Wyattville. Its dimensions are—200 feet long, 34 feet wide, 32 feet high. Through thirteen lofty and well-proportioned windows the guests may look out on the Great Quadrangle. On the opposite side are arranged, with military trophies glittering between them, portraits of James I. and Charles I., by Vandyck; Charles II. and James

II., by Sir Peter Lely; William III., Mary II., Anne, and George I., by Sir Godfrey Kneller; George II., by Zeeman; George III., by Dupont; and George IV., by Sir Thomas Lawrence. The arms of the sovereigns of the Order of the Garter, from Edward III. to William IV., are blazoned on four-and-twenty shields behind the throne or chair of state; and the arms of all the knights, from the institution of the Order to the present time, are painted on the Gothic ceiling. A music gallery is placed at either end; and on the south side four figures in complete armour (one of which represents Edward III. and another the Black Prince) "gloomily glare."

The Guard Chamber, 78 feet long, 31 feet high, and 21 to 26 feet wide, is in the Gothic style, and has a good groined roof (in plaster). Military trophies abound: of

WINDSOR, FROM THE EAST APPROACH.

special interest are the small flags annually presented by the lords of Blenheim and Strathfieldsaye in satisfaction of the tenure on which those historic demesnes are held. The armour of the Duke of Brunswick (date 1530), of Lord Howard of Effingham (1588), Queen Elizabeth's Earl of Essex (1591), Henry Prince of Wales, the "English Marcellus" (1612), Charles I. when Prince of Wales (1620), and Prince Rupert (1635), is exhibited upon life-sized figures, forming an agreeable commentary upon Sir Samuel Meyrick; while all around and about breastplates and helms, targes and shining weapons, recall the pomp and circumstance of war. On a pedestal wrought out of a shot-torn fragment of the "Victory" rests Chantrey's colossal bust of Nelson, flanked by Sevier's bust of Marlborough on one side, and Chantrey's of Wellington on the other; the three forming a group of heroes unrivalled for their "deeds of arms." Reference must also be made—though we do not profess to supply a *Catalogue Raisonné*, exhaustive and minute, of all that is to be seen, wondered at, or admired—to the two pieces of ordnance taken by Lord Cornwallis at the storming of Seringapatam, and the brass guns captured by Lord Hardinge during his brilliant campaign on the Sutlej. There are numerous other objects of interest, and many memorable relics; but the foremost work of art is the celebrated shield executed by the vain-glorious artist-silversmith Benvenuto Cellini, and presented by Francis I. to Henry VIII. on the Field of the Cloth of Gold.

"In the Armoury," says Washington Irving, "which is a Gothic Hall, furnished with weapons of various kinds and ages, I was shown a coat of armour hanging against the wall which once belonged to James the First of Scotland." We have already told the tale of the Scotch King's passion for the Lady Joan Beaufort; but the reader may not be unwilling to peruse the reflections which it suggested to the American essayist. "The suit of armour hanging up in the Hall," he says, "richly gilt and embellished as if to figure in the tourney, brought the image of the gallant and romantic prince vividly before my imagination. I paced the deserted chambers where he had composed his poem; I leaned upon the window, and endeavoured to persuade myself it was the very one where he had been visited by his vision; I looked out upon the spot where he had first seen the Lady Joan. It was the same genial and joyous month; the birds were vying with each other in strains of liquid melody; everything was bursting into vegetation, and budding forth the tender passion of the year. Time, which delights to obliterate the sterner memorials of human pride, seems to have passed lightly over this little scene of poetry and love, and to have withheld his destroying hand. Several centuries have gone by, yet the garden still flourishes at the foot of the Tower. . . . . Others may dwell on the illustrious deeds of James as a warrior and a legislator; but I have delighted to view him merely as the companion of his fellow-men; the benefactor of the human heart, stooping from his high estate to sow the sweet flowers of poetry and song in the paths of common life. He was the first to cultivate the vigorous and hardy plant of Scottish genius, which has since become so prolific of the most wholesome and highly-flavoured fruit. He carried with him into the sterner regions of the North all the fertilising arts of Southern refinement. He did everything in his power to win his countrymen to the gay, the gallant, and the gentle arts, which soften and refine the character of a people, and wreathe a grace round the loftiness of a proud and warlike spirit. . . . He contributed greatly to improve the national music; and traces of his tender sentiment and elegant taste are said to exist in those witching airs still fixed among the wild mountains and lonely glens of Scotland. He has thus connected his image with whatever is most gracious and endearing in the national character; he has embalmed his memory in song, and floated his name to after-ages in the rich streams of Scottish melody."

Lastly, we enter the Queen's Presence Chamber, where we see more Gobelin tapestry, and the "old familiar faces" of Esther, Haman, Mordecai, and Ahasuerus reappear on its elaborately woven surface; more portraits (observe Mignard's portrait of the vivacious and beautiful Henrietta of Orleans, daughter of Charles I.); and yet another of Verrio's gaudy ceilings, with Catherine of Braganza as the centre of all the Virtues—company to which her husband's Court had certainly not accustomed her; Justice engaged in the expulsion of Envy, Hatred, and Discord; and Fame proclaiming the happiness of the country blessed with Charles II. for King.

Orders of admission to the Queen's Private Apartments are rarely granted, and a detailed description of them would be an impertinence. We shall confine ourselves, therefore, to a few notes.

WINDSOR, FROM CLEWER.

The Rubens Room, or King's Drawing-Room, which is fitted up with equal taste and magnificence, commands a noble view of the North Terrace and the laughing landscape beyond. It abounds in artistic treasures, its principal decorations being the masterpieces of the great Flemish painter whose name it bears. These include—the artist's own portrait, which has been so often engraved; the portrait of Helena Fourment, the beautiful girl, his first wife's niece, whom he married in her sixteenth year; St. Martin dividing his cloak with the Beggar; the Holy Family, with St. Francis of Asrisi introduced; Philip IV. of Spain, on horseback, receiving the palm of Victory; the Archduke Albrecht of Austria, on horseback; and two grandly painted landscapes (7 ft. 7 in. wide, and 5 ft. high), known as "Summer" and "Winter," which confirm the dictum of Sir Joshua Reynolds

PRIVATE STATE-ROOMS.

that "Rubens is, perhaps, the greatest master in the mechanical part of the art, the best workman with his tools that ever exercised a pencil." The group of Sir Balthazar Gerbier and his family is in the Rubens style, though now generally attributed to Vandyck.

The King's Closet contains some good paintings by Van Cleef, Sir Antonio More, Gaspar Poussin, Jan Steen, Wouvermanns, and Steenwyck; also, "The Woman of Samaria," by Guercino; "Holy Family," Tintoretto; and "Mary Magdalen anointing the Saviour's feet," Rubens.

The Queen's Closet has for its special gem the famous "Misers," or "Money-Changers," which Quentin Matsys painted as the price of the hand of his master's daughter. There are also landscapes by Claude, interiors by Teniers, portraits by Holbein, and specimens of Rembrandt, Rubens, Titian, and others.

In the Council Chamber we observe one of Guercino's "Sibyls;" a landscape, with figure of St. John Baptist, by Correggio; Annibal Caracci's "Silence: Virgin and Child, with St. John Baptist approaching;" and Kneller's "Duke of Marlborough."

The Throne-Room can boast of some of Grinling Gibbons's delicate carving, which tempts us to pronounce him, as Evelyn does, "the greatest master, both for invention and rareness of work, that the world had in any age;" besides portraits of George III., by Gainsborough; George IV., by Sir T. Lawrence; and William IV., by Sir M. A. Shee—a *descending* scale in the quality of the painting.

The more strictly private State-rooms are approached from the Corridor, which measures 520 feet in length, and by right of its numerous busts, portraits, landscapes, and cabinets, forms an Art Gallery of rare excellence and interest. The North Corridor is, moreover, a perfect museum of precious relics and curiosities; such as the swords of Columbus, Charles I., John Hampden, King John Sobieski; the golden tiger's head, with teeth of crystal, which served as the footstool of Tippoo Saib's throne, and the jewel-studded peacock which flashed from the point of his umbrella. The Queen's Drawing-Room was the scene of the deaths of George IV. and William IV. The White Drawing-Room, now used as a breakfast-room, contains portraits of the Queen, the Prince Consort, and the Prince of Wales, by Winterhalter, a German portrait-painter, formerly patronised, much beyond his merits, by the English Court. In the Queen's Boudoir are kept the splendid cradle in which the royal children were nursed; statues of the four eldest, represented as the Four Seasons; a silver statuette of the Prince Consort in his uniform as Colonel of the 11th Hussars; and a delicately coloured china work-box, Louis Philippe's last present to the Queen. The Private Dining-Room contains the elaborate wine-cooler made for George III. at a cost of £10,500, and the splendid service of gold plate, valued at nearly £250,000.

Busts of the following persons and personages, the great by virtue of their rank and the great by virtue of their genius, are to be found in the Corridor:—Queen Anne, George I., George II., George III., George IV., William IV., and Queen Victoria, with King Ferdinand of Portugal; Prince Albert, Prince George of Cumberland, Prince George of Cambridge; the Imperial Princess of Germany and the Princess Charlotte; the Dukes of

York, Kent, Cumberland, Cambridge, and Gloucester—of Wellington, Bedford, Devonshire, and Gordon, and George Villiers, Duke of Buckingham; Marquis of Granby, Marquis of Anglesea; Earl of Harcourt, Earl Grey, Earl of Moira; Countess of Charlemont; Lords Castlereagh, Lake, Melbourne, Erskine, Ellenborough, Granville, Ligonier, Thurlow; Sir Robert Peel, Sir Thomas Hardy, Sir Isaac Newton, Sir Richard Keate, Sir Jeffry Wyattville; Archbishop Markham; Pope Pius VII.; Cardinal Gonsalvi; Marshal Blucher, Count Platoff; Shakespeare, Bacon, Locke, Boyle, Garrick, Pope, Dr. Johnson, Handel, Pitt, Fox, Sheridan, &c.

Of the royal apartments generally, a just opinion is conveyed in the following words:—"They will not indeed vie in costliness of decoration and extravagance of ornament with many of the Continental palaces; there is here no lavish expenditure, and but little of that 'display' which excites more of wonder than admiration; but there is an elegant 'fitness' in all things, appertaining more to comfort than to grandeur, and belonging less to the palace than 'the home.' But in furnishing and decoration, in the several chambers for state purposes, and in all they contain, there is amply sufficient to make the subject satisfied that the sovereign is worthily 'lodged' when at Windsor, to rejoice that it is so, and fervently to pray that so it may côntinue to be through many generations yet to come."

How shall we recount the treasures of the Plate-Room, the Royal Library, the Print-Room? We have no space to do justice to so varied and interesting a theme, and instead of attempting to point out all there is to be seen, we must be content to indicate what the privileged visitor must on no account omit to notice. The gold and silver plate, cups, vases, candelabra, salvers, shields, are remarkable alike for richness and beauty; but no description could give any possible idea of their character. The exquisite Nautilus shell, set in gold, of Benvenuto Cellini, and the highly-wrought Achilles shield of Flaxman—that shield by Homer's Hephaistos fashioned

"Vast and strong,
With rich adornment; circled with a rim,
Three-fold, bright-gleaming, whence a silver belt
Depended; of five folds the shield was formed;
And on its surface many a rare design
Of curious art his practised skill had wrought" (*Iliad* xviii.)—

are two objects of art which cannot be overlooked—"things of beauty," to which the memory will constantly recur with pleasure. Then, for historical interest, we may select the silver wine-fountain which formed part of the spoils of the Spanish Armada, the golden bellows which belonged to fair and frail Nell Gwynne, the salver engraved with the arms of Elizabeth of Bohemia, and the cup made of Spanish dollars captured at the Havannah in 1702.

In the Royal Library, founded by William IV. on a truly royal scale, but owing its present admirable arrangement and completeness to the taste and labour of the Queen and the Prince Consort, the student and the virtuoso would find ample material for years of thought and observation. The forty thousand printed books—what shall we say of them? or of the valuable MSS., including the Stuart Papers; or of the collection of drawings and English historical prints, which is probably without superior or equal? Every artist of note is represented in it; and the specimens of Leonardo da Vinci, Holbein, Michael Angelo, and Raphael, are almost unrivalled in number and excellence. The Raphael Cabinet was the idea of the Prince Consort, and consists of engravings or photographs illustrating the life, time, and work of the great Master whom the Italians, with pardonable exaggeration, call *Il Divino*. They are all uniformly mounted, bound up in volumes, and preserved in a cabinet designed and made for the purpose by Mr. Crace.

Of drawings by Holbein there are 87; by Raphael, 53 (but all are not indisputably genuine); and there are numerous specimens of Albert Durer, Lucas Cranach, Nicolas Poussin, Claude Lorraine, Fra Bartolommeo, Guido, Andrea del Sarto, Guercino, Dominichino, Titian, Tintoretto, Correggio, Luca Signorelli, Fra Filippo Lippi, and others.

Here we take leave of Windsor, having said enough, we hope, to assist the reader to a just conception of the historic interest, architectural magnificence, and artistic treasures of the one royal palace that is really worthy of imperial England; that has "grown with the growth of the nation, and accommodated itself to its progress; that has advanced with it from the rude strength and suspicious defences of the feudal days, through the struggles of early civilisation, to the present calm display of greatness and refinement, of power and wealth."

SPANISH WINE-FLAGON.   SEE P. 119.

ETON COLLEGE

BURNHAM BEECHES.—SEE PAGE 143.

CHAPTER XII.

ETON COLLEGE.

FROM Windsor we cross the river to Eton, the most famous of our public schools; the one which, on the whole, has exercised the greatest influence on the training and education of our "upper classes."

We suppose everybody knows that "the College of the Blessed Marie of Eton beside Wyndesore" was founded by Henry VI., as a nursery for the new foundation of King's College which he had established at Cambridge. The foundation charter, dated September 12, 1440, is still preserved. The charter was confirmed by Parliament in May, 1441; and on the 3rd of the following July the King laid the first stone of the chapel. He continued for many years his fostering care of the institution, which he desired and designed to make the best grammar-school in England; drawing upon his own resources for its erection and endowment, and making over to it the estates of several alien priories. Of the intense interest he felt even in the minutest details of the building, his written directions afford abundant evidence. The College, he wrote, was to be constructed of "the most substantial and best abiding stuff, of stone, lead, glass, and iron, that may goodly be had and provided thereto." He described the plan of the chapel, which was to surpass the New College Chapel at

Oxford, and specified its dimensions; and this with a minuteness which left little to the invention of the architect. The boundary of the College was to measure 3590 feet in circumference, and its walls were to extend from the high-road on the east to the river on the west. The principal gateway, on the north-west, was to give access to the outer quadrangle; on the right side of which was to rise an almshouse, containing sixteen rooms, besides kitchen, buttery, and offices; and on the left, the infirmary, bakehouse, brewery, stables, "with chambres for the stewardes, auditores, and other lerned counsell and ministres of the said College," were to be erected. A second gateway, opening into the main quadrangle, was to be surmounted by a fine tower, the interior of which was to be appropriated as a treasury and muniment-room. The area of the great quadrangle was to measure 155 feet north and south, and 230 feet east and west, and to be surrounded by buildings of one story above the ground, with a series of small projecting towers on both sides. Many of the towers were intended as staircases to the upper rooms, as it was not designed to have any corridors. On the west side of the court, with a pleasant view of the gardens and river, was to be placed the library; the hall and pantry were to occupy their present positions on the south. The Provost's lodging was to extend for a length of seventy feet on both floors, from a point behind the upper end of the hall to a corner tower situated close to the northeast angle of the new church. Exactly opposite, on the ground floor, was to be a schoolroom of similar length adjoining the gateway. Finally, in the centre of the quadrangle was to stand a conduit, "goodly devised to the ease and profit of the said College." No one long dormitory was to be created; but bedrooms for the scholars, choristers, and commensals were to be provided on the ground floor, with the condition that in each room should be at least three senior scholars charged to keep order. All boys under fourteen were to sleep two in a bed. Each of the Fellows and the Head Master were to occupy separate rooms on the upper floor; while to the chaplains, usher, and clerks was assigned one room for two persons. A special caution was given to the upper-floor occupants not to inconvenience those below them by spilling wine, beer, or water. The site of the present school-yard and upper school was to be

CHURCH STAIRCASE, ETON.

occupied by an oblong cloister on the west side of the great quadrangle, which, as its most conspicuous feature, would boast a great tower, 140 feet high. This cloister was to be the scene of learned grammatical tournaments between the scholars. Here, also, would be interred the Provosts and all other members of the College down to the scholars; while, on the south side, an area of thirty-eight feet was to be planted with certain trees and flowers "behovable and convenient" for the service of the College church. Henry's energy and enthusiasm communicated itself to his subordinates; and within three years the edifices were so far advanced that possession of them was formally given to the Provost, clerks, and scholars (December 21, 1443). In choosing Fellows, Henry paid regard to their learning, we are told, rather than to their musical acquirements. If he met any of the young Etonians in Windsor Castle, on a visit to members of his household, he never failed to exhort them to walk in the pleasant ways of virtue, and presenting them with a small gift of money, would say :—"Be good boys, meek and docile, and servants of the Lord." The outbreak of the Wars of the Roses, however, threw a fatal shadow over Henry's later reign, and the College made no further progress. Its educational work, however, had been well begun under the direction of William of Waynflete (afterwards Bishop of Winchester), who had removed thither from Winchester School, taking with him five Fellows and thirty-five scholars.

It was hardly to be expected, perhaps, that Edward IV. should bestow his patronage on his predecessor's favourite foundation; but it would have been generous if he had not wreaked upon it his revenge. After seizing a considerable portion of its revenues for his own use, and plundering it of "moveables of great value," he conceived the idea of merging it into St. George's of Windsor, and obtained a papal bull for that purpose. He was foiled, however, by Westbury, who had succeeded Waynflete as Provost, and displayed a tenacity and a resolution the King could not but respect. He contented himself, therefore, with conferring some of its lands on the college of Fotheringham in Northamptonshire. So heavy were the blows thus inflicted upon it, that its revenues sunk from £1500 a-year to £370; a sum inadequate to meet the annual expenses. Economy, therefore, on the most rigid scale, had to be adopted; the vacant Fellowships were not filled up, the almsmen were abolished, and the number of scholars considerably reduced. Gradually the College recovered the royal favour and its lost ground : Edward obtained a revocation of the papal bull, and in July, 1471, visited Eton, with his queen, in state. He was there again in September, and ordered that a boat should be specially kept for his use. It is probable that his new interest in the College was aroused by the influence of his queen's eldest brother, Anthony Earl Rivers, a generous and discerning patron of literature and learned men.

William Paston, of the honourable Paston family, whose letters throw such a flood of light on men and manners in the troublous times of the later Plantagenets, was a boy at Eton in 1478-9, and from thence wrote to his elder brother on several occasions, frankly describing his love-making and verse-making. The following specimen of an Eton boy's composition, four centuries ago, will amuse the reader :—

"To his worshipful brother, John Paston, be this delivered in haste.

"RIGHT REVEREND AND WORSHIPFUL BROTHER,—After all duties of recommendation, I commend me to you, desiring to hear of your prosperity and welfare, which I pray God long to continue to His pleasure and to your heart's desire; telling you next that I received a letter from you, in the which letter was 8d., with the which I should buy a pair of slippers.

"Furthermore, certifying you as for the 13s. 4d. which you sent by a gentleman's man for my board, called Thomas Newton, was delivered to mine hostess, and so to my creansor [creditor], Mr. Thomas Stevenson [a Fellow of Eton]; and he heartily commended him to you. Also you sent me word in the letter of 12lb. of figs and 8lb. of raisins; and I have them not delivered, but I doubt not I shall have, for Aleveder told me of them, and he said that they came after in another barge.

"And as for the young gentlewoman, I will certify you how I first fell in acquaintance with her. Her father is dead; there be two sisters of them; the elder is just wedded, at which wedding I was with mine hostess and also desired by the gentleman himself, called William Swan, whose dwelling is in Eton. So it fortuned that mine hostess reported on me otherwise than I was worthy; so that her mother commanded her to make me good cheer, and so in good faith she did. She is not abiding where she is now; her dwelling is in London; but her mother and she came to a place of trees five miles from Eton, where the wedding was, for because it was nigh to the gentleman which wedded her daughter; and on Monday next coming—that is to say, the first Monday of Clean Lent—her mother and she will go to the garden at Sheen, and so push to London, and there to abide in a place of trees in Bow Churchyard. And if it please you to inquire of her, her mother's name is Mistress Alborow, the name of the daughter is Margaret Alborow; the age of her is by all likelihood eighteen, or nineteen years at the farthest; and as for the money and plate, it is ready whensoever she were wedded; but as for the livelihood, I trow, not till after her mother's decease, but I cannot tell you for very certain, but you may know by inquiring. And as for her beauty, judge you that when you see her, if so be ye take the labour, and specially behold her hands, for and if it be as is told me she is disposed to be thick (!).

"And as for my coming from Eton, I lack nothing but versifying, which I trust to have with a little continuance.

"Quare quomodo non valet hora valet mora.
Unde di [ctum est] :—*
Arbore jam videns exemplum. Non die possunt
Omnia suppleri, sed tamen illa mora.

"And these two verses aforesaid be of mine own making. No more to you at this time, but God have you in his keeping. Written at Eton, the Eve of St. Matthias the Apostle, in haste, with the hand of your brother, "WILLIAM PASTON, Junr."

---

* This line was probably a theme set by the master.

Let us hope that Master William Paston, junr., succeeded better in his love-making than in his verse-making, or he would assuredly come to grief!

No great change affected the fortunes of Eton in the reign of Henry VII. or Henry VIII. The latter was an occasional visitor to the College, but by no means a benefactor. In 1534, Nicholas Udall was appointed to the head-mastership, and through him Eton becomes temporarily connected with the development of English literature. Udall was described as "the best schoolmaster and greatest beater of our time," and for his skill and prowess in the use of the birch was renowned among his contemporaries. Thus, Thomas Tusser, the author of the "Five Hundred Points of Good Husbandry," relates, as his most unpleasant experience, that

HEAD MASTER'S ROOM, ETON COLLEGE.

> "From Paul's I went, to Eton sent,
> To learn straightways the Latin phrase,
> When fifty-three stripes given to me
> At once, I had!

> "For fault but small, or none at all,
> It came to pass thus beat I was:
> See, Udall, see, the mercy of thee
> To me, poor lad!"

But Udall was something more than schoolmaster and flagellator; he was a great patron of theatrical performances, and wrote for his boy-actors the earliest English comedy extant, "Ralph Roister Doister." This is a specimen of its style:—

> "Lord, how necessary it is, now-of-days,
> That each body live uprightly all manner ways,
> For let never so little a gap be open,
> And be sure of this, the worst shall be spoken.
> How innocent stand I in this for deed or thought,
> And yet see what mistrust towards me it hath wrought.
> But thou, Lord, knowest all folks' thoughts and intents,
> And Thou art the Deliverer of all innocents."

There are thirteen characters, and the scene is laid in London; so that, to some extent, Udall's comedy is a representation of the manners of "polite" society, and exhibits some of "the peculiarities of thinking and acting" in the metropolis at the time when it was written.

At the dissolution of the colleges and charities, in the reign of Edward VI., Eton was specially exempted; its revenues were then estimated to produce £1101 yearly.

During the reign of Mary, the Provost and Fellows accommodated themselves to the religious reaction which she had favoured, repairing the high altar, replacing the bason for holy water in its old position near the church door, and expelling such of the Fellows as had taken unto themselves wives. The manner of life then practised by the Etonians has been carefully detailed by Mr. Maxwell Lyte, and presents some noteworthy features. At five the boys were awakened by one of the præpostors, who thundered forth the word of ill omen, *Surgite*. While dressing, they chanted their prayers, and thus economised time. Each boy made his own bed, and swept the dust from under it into the middle of the Long Chamber, whence the accumulation was removed by four juniors. The next process was washing, which was performed at the pump in couples. Cleansed and refreshed, the boys repaired to the schoolroom; the usher made his appearance at six; and prayers were said, after which a præposter examined the juvenile hands and faces, in order to report the *immundani* to the head master. That illustrious personage entered at seven o'clock, and studies lasted until about nine. Then, breakfast. At ten, the boys returned to the schoolroom; more prayers; more work; and at eleven, dinner, the boys marching thither and returning in double file. Lessons were resumed at mid-day, and continued until three. From three to four was given up to recreation; from four to five the boys were again in the schoolroom; supper followed; and from six to eight the next day's lessons were prepared. At eight the boys went to bed, chanting prayers. There seems, in this statement, an indifferent proportion of play; but holidays were not infrequent, and in summer the leisure time was considerably extended.

The scholars of Eton vied with poets and courtiers in pouring the tribute of an enthusiastic loyalty at the feet of Queen Elizabeth. Among the MS. treasures of the British Museum is preserved a small volume of Latin verses, comprising the productions of forty-four boys in the upper forms, differing considerably in quality and quantity, but resembling one another in their expression of the most absolute devotion. This bears date about 1559-1560. Another belongs to the year 1563, and is interesting from its containing effusions by Giles Fletcher, afterwards Ambassador to Russia, and Longe, afterwards Archbishop of Armagh. Many of the verses can be read backwards as well as forwards; others assume the form of acrostics. Elizabeth is likened to Abraham, Moses, Aaron, Gideon, Samson, Samuel, and Judith; while all the goddesses of the ancient mythology are deprived of their special gifts for her royal adornment.

> "Nempe Minerva, Venus Juno. tibi munera clara
> Distribuunt. corpus Venus eximium, tibi Juno
> Divitias Arabum gazas gemmasque nitentes,
> Virtutem Pallas quæ non peritura vigebit."

The French hostages surrendered to England as security for the performance of the conditions of the Treaty of Cambray were, strangely enough, lodged at Eton. According to Froude, they amused themselves with misleading the Eton boys into iniquity; they brought ambiguous damsels into the Fellows' Common Room, and in the Fellows' precincts behaved "in an unseemly manner." In 1564, however, Eton got rid of them; they were thrown into prison in retaliation for the arrest of Throckmorton, the English Ambassador.

Late in the reign of Elizabeth, Sir Henry Savile, Warden of Merton College, whom Hallam styles "the most learned Englishman in profane literature of his time," and who was certainly not less profoundly versed in theological knowledge, was elected Provost. He held both posts to the day of his death; and thus "the skilful gardener," as Fuller quaintly says, "had at the same time a nursery of young Plants and an Orchard of grown Trees, both flourishing under his carefull inspection." The Queen paid two visits to Eton during his Provostship, namely, in 1596 and 1601. He fell into disgrace with her imperious Majesty through his close friendship with the Earl of Essex; was arrested; but, after a short detention in private custody, released. In the same year he splendidly welcomed, at Eton, De Biron, the French Ambassador, who arrived with a great retinue. In 1603, the "bright occidental star" having set, Eton paid homage to James I., who knighted its Provost. In reference to this honour, Lady Savile remarked that it came too late, and therefore was not worthy of her. She is described as a woman of discontented temper, who was jealous of the time Sir Henry bestowed upon his literary studies. "I would I were a book too," she once remarked, "and then, Sir Henry, you would a little more respect me." A bystander ungallantly rejoined:—"Then, madam, you must be an almanack, that he might change you every year." Sir Henry's literary reputation rests upon his treatise on Roman warfare, his share in the revision of the Bible, and his superb edition of Chrysostom; the last, an enduring monument of his scholarship. His labours on this great work so seriously injured his health, that Lady Savile declared she would burn Chrysostom for killing her husband.

In spite of the saying of the Latin poet, learning does not *always* soften the manners; and this great scholar was as austere as he was erudite. He would fain have been thought equal to Scaliger, and was visibly agitated when free eulogiums were lavished on other scholars. "It is his custom," said Casaubon, "to kick all men who are generally reputed learned, and to treat them as asses on two legs." He was unpopular at Eton on account of his severity of discipline. Of clever boys who would not work, but trusted to their natural talents to pull them through, he cherished a strong dislike. "Give me," he would say, "the plodding student. If I would look for wits I would go to Newgate; there be the wits;"—an epigrammatic saying which conveyed only half a truth. Under his rule, however, Eton flourished mightily. At the election of 1613, there were upwards of a hundred candidates for admission, and the Provost was worried with solicitations from anxious parents all over England. This prosperous condition endured until his death in February, 1621–2.

He was succeeded by one Thomas Murray, whom disease carried off in fourteen months. A prolonged and vigorous competition for the vacant office then ensued; Lord Bacon, Sir Henry Wotton, and Sir Dudley Carleton being among the candidates. Wotton was successful; and his administration of the College fully justified the appointment. Izaak Walton, in his admirable biography of his friend, speaks of him as "a constant cherisher of all those youths in that school in whom he found either a constant diligence or a genius that prompted them to learning," and as "pleased constantly to breed up one or more hopeful youths, which he picked out of the school, and took into his own domestic care, and to attend him at his meals." Not only a fine gentleman himself, but well skilled in the art of making others so, "he would never leave the school without dropping some choice Greek or Latin apothegm or sentence, such as were worthy of a room in the memory of a growing scholar." "He used specially to urge the boys not to neglect rhetoric, because Almighty God hath left mankind affections to be wrought upon." "He caused to be choicely drawn the pictures of divers of the most famous Greek and Latin historians, poets, and orators," and these he set up in the school, with the view of exciting in the boys a deeper interest in their works.

In 1639, Richard Stewart, Clerk of the Closet to Charles I., was elected to the Provostship. Clarendon characterises him as a very honest and learned gentleman, conversant in that learning which vindicated the dignity and authority of the Church, upon which his heart was most entirely set, "not without some prejudice to those who thought there was any other object to be more carefully pursued." In February, 1644, he was removed by the Parliament on account of his adhesion to the royal cause, and Francis Rous, by no means an incompetent person, took his place. He was zealously careful to prevent any encroachments on the service or privileges of the College. Cromwell himself was well-disposed towards it, and continued the annual royal gift of wine and venison. Rous acted as Speaker to the "Barebones Parliament," and was afterwards a member of Cromwell's short-lived House of Peers. He died in January, 1659, leaving special instructions for his interment at Eton, "a place which hath my dear affections and prayers, that it may be a flourishing nursery of piety and learning to the end of the world."

After the Restoration, Nicholas Monk, brother of Monk "the King-maker," became Provost, but enjoyed the dignity only for a few months. He was succeeded by Dr. Meredith, who died in 1665, and the post was then offered to, but declined by, Robert Boyle, who must always rank among the most eminent of the elder English men of science. Dr. Allestree, Professor of Divinity at Oxford, was finally appointed, and the latest historian of the College speaks of him as "one of the best Provosts that Eton ever had. Although," he adds, "he did not attain to the same reputation in literature and politics as several of his predecessors, he was at least equal to any of them in administrative ability." He rescued the College from the slough of financial embarrassment into which it had sunk, made a considerable addition to the buildings, and reformed the internal organisation. Another generous benefactor and skilful ruler was Henry Godolphin, brother of Queen Anne's great minister, who presided over the College from 1695 to 1732, a period illustrated by many eminent names among the scholars, as, for instance, William

QUADRANGLE OF ETON COLLEGE

Pitt ("the great Commoner"), Charles Pratt (Earl of Camden), George Lyttleton, and Henry Fox (first Lord Holland). Jacob Bryant, the mythologist, Horace Walpole, letter-writer, romancist, antiquary, and dilettante, and the poet Gray, were also Etonians of this period.

Whatever sunshine there is in the royal presence, was frequently enjoyed by Eton in the earlier and happier years of George III. He had a strong affection for the College, and took as lively an interest in its welfare as if he had been brought up within its walls. The Head Master, at the date of the King's accession, was Dr. Edward Barnard, who seems to have possessed much of Dr. Arnold's tact in dealing with boys, and a sound knowledge of their character. Mankind, as everybody knows, is divided into three classes —men, women, and boys; and it by no means follows that he who understands men and women will also understand that other and most puzzling class, the boys. Dr. Barnard, however, *did;* and hence his success as a master.

GRAY'S TOMB.—SEE PAGE 142.

Among his pupils was Charles James Fox, who owed it to his care and firmness that he was not irretrievably spoiled by parental indulgence. The genius of the future statesman was discerned not only by the sagacious head master, but by Fox's schoolfellows, one of whom, the young Earl of Carlisle, addressed him in the following prophetic lines:—

> "How will my Fox, alone, from strength of parts,
> Shake the loud senate, animate the hearts
> Of fearful statesmen, while around you stand
> Both Peers and Commons, list'ning your command!
> While Tully's muse its weight to you affords,
> His nervous sweetness shall adorn your words;
> What praise to Pitt, to Townshend, e'er was due,
> In future times, my Fox, shall wait on you."

Mr. Lyte has collected some illustrations of George III.'s partiality to Eton. When

R

De Quincey's parents had some idea of sending their boy to the famous College, the King said to him, emphatically :—" All people think highly of Eton ; everybody praises Eton. Your mother does right to inquire; there can be no harm in that; but the more she inquires, the more she will be satisfied—that I can answer for." He knew many of the boys personally, and would chat with them in the street, generally ending his colloquy with the welcome inquiry :—" Shall I get you a holiday ?" If he met with an unfamiliar face, he would stop to ask :—" What's your name ? Who is your tutor ? Who is your dame ?" and on receiving the answers, would generally observe :—" *Very* good tutor, *very* good dame." With so vigilant an eye did he watch the careers of clever and promising scholars, that on one occasion he reminded an eminent statesman of a prize he had formerly won at Eton. On Sunday afternoons the boys would assemble on the Terrace in full dress, applying, if any unfortunate holes and rents disfigured their black stockings, a judicious coating of ink. Mr. John Barnard, of King's College, remembers being present at one of these Sunday parades with his

BOAT-HOUSES, ETON.

father and brothers, more than seventy years ago. The good-natured monarch came up to them, exchanged a few kindly words with the father, and asked:—" Who is this?" " My son, sir, whom I have lately placed at Eton." " What !" said the King, with assumed severity. " Lower boy, do you know that you are out of bounds ?" Then, to the elder brother, who was in the sixth form, he said :—" Put him in the bill, præpostor ; he must be flogged !" Our wits have dealt very sharply with the royalty in undress to which George III. was prone; but, after all, it suited the time, and probably helped to confirm and quicken that loyal feeling which supported many an old institution through a period of terrible strain and pressure.

It would be unpardonable to pass from this epoch in the annals of Eton without an allusion to the first and most brilliant of Eton magazines, " The Microcosm," which was begun in 1781, and carried on until Electiontide, 1787, under the joint management of

George Canning, John Smith, Robert ("Bobus") Smith, and John Hookham Frere (afterwards the translator of "Aristophanes"). Canning's contributions were numerous; one, a poem of much merit, on "The Slavery of Greece," exhibits his liberality of sentiment and vigour of thought; another is a felicitous imitation of the old style of criticism in the shape of a commentary on the well-known nursery song—

> "The Queen of Hearts
> She made some tarts,
> All on a summer's day."

There is an abundance of cleverness in "The Microcosm;" the writing is always correct, often elegant, and the humour is neither coarse nor artificial. Its authors seem to have been well known; for in 1787, Miss Burney (the author of "Evelina") attended the Royal Family on a visit to Eton to hear the speeches; and she tells us in her Diary that they "were chiefly in Greek and Latin, but concluded with three or four in English; some were pronounced extremely well, especially those spoken by the chief composers of the 'Microcosm,' Canning and Smith."

"The Microcosm" has had many successors, of which the most successful was "The Etonian," started by a genius scarcely less brilliant, if less comprehensive, than Canning— Winthrop Mackworth Praed. Some of the best of his admirable *vers de société* and character-sketches, such as "Surley Hall," "The County Ball," and "Laura," appeared in its pages. He was assisted by William Sidney Walker, John Moultrie, a poet of no mean order, and Henry Nelson Coleridge, whose amiable character and great abilities are affectionately recorded by his widow, Sara Coleridge, in the autobiography prefixed to her "Memoir and Letters." Another contributor was "Richard Durnford," the present Bishop of Chichester. The four young penmen afterwards combined with Macaulay, Derwent Coleridge, and Henry Malden to produce a London serial, the once famous though brief-lived "Knight's Quarterly Magazine," the story of which is pleasantly told by Mr. Trevelyan in his "Life of Lord Macaulay."

From Praed's "Surley Hall," we extract a passage descriptive of Etonian aquatics :—

> "The sun hath shed a mellowed beam,
> Fair Thames, upon thy silver stream,
> And air and water, earth and heaven,
> Lie in the calm repose of even.
> How silently the breeze moves on,
> Flutters and whispers, and is gone !
> How calmly does the quiet sky
> Sleep in its cold serenity !
> Alas ! how sweet a scene were here
> For shepherd, or for sonnetteer;
> How fit the place, how fit the time,
> For making love, or making rhyme !
> But though the sun's descending ray
> Smiles warmly on the close of day,

> 'Tis not to gaze upon his light
> That Eton's sons are here to-night;
> And though the river, calm and clear,
> Makes music to the poet's ear,
> 'Tis not to listen to the sound
> That Eton's sons are thronging round:
> The sun unheeded may decline—
> Blue eyes send out a brighter shine;
> The wave may cease its gurgling moan —
> Glad voices have a sweeter tone;
> For in our calendar of bliss
> We have no hour so gay as this,
> When the kind hearts and brilliant eyes
> Of those we know and love and prize,
> Are come to cheer the captive's thrall,
> And smile upon his festival."

It must be owned that these are smoothly and fancifully written lines for a lad of seventeen. They exhibit all the characteristics of Praed's mature style. Here is another specimen :—

> " Father Thames beholds to-night
> A thousand visions of delight;
> Tearing and swearing, jeering, cheering,
> Lame steeds to right and left careering,
> Displays, dismays, disputes, distresses,
> Ruffling of temper and of dresses;
> Wounds on the heart—and on the knuckles;
> Losing of patience—and of buckles. . . .
>
> " Lord! what would be the Cynic's mirth,
> If Fate would lift him to the earth,
> And set his tub, with magic jump,
> Squat down beside the Brocas clump! . . .
> And then the badges and the boats,
> The flags, the drums, the paint, the coats;
> But more than these, and more than all,
> The puller's intermitted call—
> ' Easy!'—' Hard all !'—' Now pick her up !'
> ' Upon my life, how I shall sup !'—
> Would be a fine and merry matter
> To wake the sage's love of satire."

William IV., we are told, was not less partial to Eton than George III. had been, and was wont to attend the speeches on the 4th of June, or on Easter Monday, every year. On the second of these visits, in 1832, he promised the reversion of the Provostship to Eton's celebrated head master, Dr. Keate, in his characteristically blunt fashion. Pointing to Dr. Goodall, he said, "When he goes, I'll make you him." (Kings are *super grammaticam !*) Dr. Keate wisely held his tongue; but the Provost, a gentleman of high spirit and fine manners, bowed in his courtliest manner, and replied, " Sire, I could never think of *going* before your Majesty." The Eton boys returned the royal favour by demonstrations of effusive loyalty. In one of the annual addresses delivered before King William in the Upper School, George Smythe, afterwards a prominent founder of the "Young England" party, and the hero of Lord Beaconsfield's "Coningsby," adroitly connected him with his royal father in a warm tribute of gratitude :—

> "Thou (like thy sire) on us art pleased to bend
> The gracious looks of Patron, Father, Friend,
> Till in thy cheering smile consoled we see
> Another George—our loved, our lost—in thee."

Nor was the Queen forgotten.

> "Inspired by thee, oh, long may England's fair
> Look to the throne, and find examples there;
> And copying thee, and thus resistless made,
> Still reign o'er subject hearts like Adelaide."

Coming down to the present reign, we note as interesting incidents the gorgeous illuminations on the occasion of the Queen's marriage in 1840; the visit of the King of Prussia in 1842; that of Louis Philippe in 1844, when he was accompanied by the Queen, Prince Albert, and the Duke of Wellington; and the funeral of that illustrious Etonian, the Marquis Wellesley, who, by his own express desire, was buried at Eton. Great changes have taken place of late years in the organisation, the social life, the discipline, and even the curriculum of the College, but none of these have injuriously affected its character or prosperity. It is well that it should be so, for all England is concerned in the welfare of Eton, the largest, wealthiest, and most famous of her public schools. "In spite of drawbacks and many deficiencies, it can boast," as its enthusiastic historian says, "a glorious past. In the church and in the senate, at the bar and in the army, and in every other branch of national life, her sons have held their own, and left their mark. At Eton have been learned the early lessons of endurance, patience, self-control, and sturdy independence which have braced the characters of England's greatest men. In that world in miniature the boy has been taught to find his own level, and to respect his fellows and himself—lessons happily remembered longer than much of his school work. If university honours and numbers on the school-list are any signs of success, there is no evidence of decay at Eton."

One of Eton's most characteristic privileges was abolished in 1847. This was the triennial celebration of what was known as the "Eton Montem," the object of which was to raise a sum of money called "salt-money" for presentation to the senior scholar, or "Captain" of the school, on his removal to King's College, Cambridge. On these occasions a very bright and amusing scene took place. The scholars, attired in fanciful uniforms of their own devising, and led by a marshal, colonels, and other officers, marched to an elevated spot called Salt Hill ("ad Montem"), just beyond Slough, on the Bath road, where, amidst certain traditional formalities, they waved a flag. It was customary for the festival to be attended by large numbers of the higher classes, as well as by old Etonians and friends of the scholars, and upon each a contribution was levied. The "salt," collected by a couple of "salt-bearers," assisted by "scouts," frequently amounted to a considerable total, seldom less than £1000, and sometimes rising to £1400. Carrying out the ancient practice, the salt-bearers were accustomed to provide themselves with a handkerchief full of salt, a small quantity of which they bestowed on every individual contributing to their treasure-chest. It was a favourite joke, in the days when George III. was king, for the salt-bearers to fill with this commodity the mouth of any stolid-looking rustic who, after giving them a trifle, seemed to expect an equivalent.

A brilliant description of this picturesque, but not altogether edifying festival occurs in the early pages of Lord Beaconsfield's "Coningsby." "On this day," he says, "the Captain of Eton appears in a dress as martial as his title; indeed each boy represents in his uniform—though not, perhaps, according to the exact rules of the Horse Guards—an officer of the army. One is a marshal, another an ensign. There is a lieutenant, too, and the remainder are sergeants. Each of those who are invested with these ephemeral commissions has one or more attendants, the number of these varying according to his rank. These servitors are selected according to the wishes of the several members of the sixth form, out of the ranks of the lower boys, that is, those boys who are below the fifth form; and all these attendants are arrayed in a variety of fancy dresses. The Captain of the Oppidans, and the Senior Colleger next to the Captain of the School, figure also in fancy costume, and are called 'Salt-bearers.' It is their business, together with the twelve senior collegers of the fifth form, who are called 'Runners,' and whose costume is also determined by the taste of the wearers, to levy the contributions. And all the Oppidans of the sixth form class as 'Corporals,' and are severally followed by one or more lower boys, who are denominated 'Polemen,' but who appear in their ordinary dress." This passage must now be read in the past tense; but no doubt the ceremony it describes fully justified, in its prime, the declaration of "Madame Colonna," that "she had met nothing in England equal to Montem; that it was a Protestant carnival; and that its only fault was that it did not last forty days." It belonged, however, both in spirit and substance, to a past order of things; and its abolition was as inevitable as the abolition of "rotten boroughs."

Henry VI.'s foundation included a provost, ten priests, four lay clerks, six choristers, twenty-five poor grammar scholars, with a master to teach them, and twenty-five bedesmen, bound to offer up prayers for the King. The present establishment consists of a provost, seven fellows (one of whom is vice-provost), head master, under master, and three conducts, seven clerks, ten lay clerks, seventy "King's scholars," and ten choristers. There are also 700 to 800 scholars ("Oppidans") *not* on the foundation. The prizes to which Etonians may aspire are four scholarships at King's College, Cambridge (given annually), two "postmasterships" at Merton College, Oxford, and about forty benefices. The majority, however, belong to a class whose youth—the "gilded youth" of English society—stand in need of no such rewards. They are attracted to Eton by its ancient repute, its long-established prestige, and its social distinction. And whatever defects, if any, still cling to its administration, who will deny that it deserves the renown it has attained, and fully justifies the affection with which it is regarded by its sons?

"That delicious plain," exclaims Lord Beaconsfield, "studded with every creation of graceful culture; hamlet, and hall, and grange; garden, and grove, and park; that castle-palace, grey with glorious ages; those antique spires, hoar with faith and wisdom; the chapel and the college; that river winding through the shady meads; the sunny glade and the solemn avenue; the room in the Dame's house where we first order our own breakfast, and first feel we are free; the stirring multitude, the energetic groups, the individual mind that leads, conquers, controls; the emulation and the affection; the noble strife and the tender sentiment; the daring exploit and the dashing scrape; the passion that pervades our life and breathes in everything, from the aspiring study to the inspiring sport—oh! what hereafter can spur the brain and touch the heart like this; can give us a world so deeply and variously interesting; a life so full of quick and bright excitement —passed in a scene so fair?"

Feelings not dissimilar, and an affection equally strong, appear in Gray's fine verses "On a Distant Prospect of Eton College;" and that we may have done with our quotations, we shall here introduce three or four illustrative stanzas:—

> "Ye distant spires, ye antique towers,
> That crown the watery glade,
> Where grateful Science still adores
> Her Henry's holy shade;*
> And ye, that from the stately brow
> Of Windsor's heights, th' expanse below
> Of grove, of lawn, of mead survey,
> Whose turf, whose shade, whose flowers among,
> Wanders the hoary Thames along
> His silver-winding way.
>
> "Ah, happy hills!† ah, pleasing shade!
> Ah, fields belov'd in vain!
> Where once my careless childhood stray'd,
> A stranger yet to pain!
> I feel the gales that from ye blow
> A momentary bliss bestow;
> As waving fresh their gladsome wing
> My weary soul they seem to soothe,
> And, redolent of joy and youth,
> To breathe a second spring.
>
> "Say, Father Thames, for thou hast seen
> Full many a sprightly race,
> Disporting on thy margent green,
> The paths of pleasure trace;

---

* A reminiscence of Shakespeare's "Holy Henry."
† The emendation, "rills," has been suggested, and certainly there are no hills near Eton.

Who foremost now delight to cleave,
With pliant arm, thy glossy wave?
The captive linnet which enthral?
What idle progeny succeed
To chase the rolling circle's speed,
Or urge the flying ball? . .

"Gay hope is theirs by fancy fed,
Less pleasing when possest ;
The tear forgot as soon as shed,
The sunshine of the breast :
Theirs buxom health of rosy hue,
Wild wit, invention ever new,
And lively cheer, of vigour born ;
The thoughtless day, the easy night,
The spirits pure, the slumbers light,
That fly the approach of morn."

The College buildings consist of two quadrangles, in one of which are the chapel, school, and dormitory of the foundation-scholars ; in the other, the library, provost's and masters' houses, and the lodgings of the fellows. The chapel is built of Caen stone ; the remainder of the old buildings of dark red brick, with stone dressings, and clustered chimney shafts of the substantial character to which we are accustomed in Tudor edifices. Through a central gateway the visitor enters the first quadrangle, or "School Yard," and sees before him the tall structure of the Clock Tower. On his right is the beautiful chapel ; the school buildings occupy the other three sides of the quadrangle, and a bronze statue of Henry VI., by Bird, adorns the centre. The Lower School is on the north side ; above it is the old dormitory, or "Long Chamber," so famous in Etonian chronicles, but now broken up into separate apartments. On the west side is the Upper School, which was erected by Sir Christopher Wren.

LOWER SCHOOL, ETON.

The Chapel closely resembles in character that of King's College, Cambridge ; but it is, of course, on a smaller scale, and less elaborate in construction. By its founder it was intended only to serve as the choir of the stately structure which he contemplated. Its length is 175 feet. In 1848 to 1860 it was very carefully restored under the superintendence of Mr. H. Woodyer ; the windows were then filled with good painted glass of excellent design and colouring, and oak stalls and seats took the place of the shabby benches in which so many generations of Etonians had sat. The interior is rendered specially interesting by its monuments and memorials of departed provosts and head masters, including Sir Henry Wotton, Francis Rous, and Dr. Allestree, who erected the Upper School. There is also a monument to a famous Etonian who did the State good service, the Marquis Wellesley. The ante-chapel, or Chantry Chapel, on the north, was founded by Provost Lupton, *temp.* Henry VII. Observe his rebus, a tern with the word "Lup" above it, carved over the door. The chapel contains his tomb, and a statue of Henry VI. by Bacon.

The graveyard exhibits some traces of the old parish church, which was removed by Henry VI. to make space for his College chapel. Here lies buried the "ever memorable" Hales. John Hales, one of the rational or moderate theologians of the sixteenth century, was born at Bath, in 1584. He was educated in his native city in "grammar learning;" and at 13 years of age entered a scholar of Corpus Christi College, where he took his degree in July, 1603. "The prodigous pregnancy of his parts" procured him a Fellowship at Merton College in 1605. In 1612 he was appointed to the Greek Professorship, and in May, 1614, admitted a Fellow of Eton. We find him, in 1618-19, attending the Synod of Dort, and taking part in its proceedings. Returning to England, he settled down to the enjoyment of his learned leisure at Eton, where he maintained an active correspondence with Chillingworth, and formed friendly relations with Ben Jonson, Sir John Suckling, Lord Falkland, and other wits, poets, and thinkers. Suckling, in some pleasant lines, refers to their occasional meetings :—

> "There you shall find the wit and wine
> Flowing alike, and both divine;
> Dishes, with names not known in books,
> And less amongst the college cooks;
> With sauce so pregnant, that you need
> Not stay till hunger bids you feed.
> The sweat of learnéd Jonson's brain,
> And gentle Shakespeare's easier strain,
> A hackney coach conveys you to,
> In spite of all that rain can do :
> And for your eighteenpence you sit
> The lord and judge of all fresh wit."

Hales, however, devoted but a small portion of his time to this lively intercourse. He lived chiefly among his books; in the intervals of his studies enjoying the learned companionship of two successive provosts, Sir Henry Savile and Sir Henry Wotton. His controversial work began shortly before, or soon after, the death of the latter, and soon assumed importance. An attentive circle of readers welcomed his tracts on "Schism," "Concerning the Power of the Keys," and "On the Sacrament of the Lord's Supper." Their liberal vein of thought was not grateful to the ecclesiastical authorities of the time, and their learned and gentle-minded writer received, therefore, no other Church preferment than a Canonry of Windsor. During the troubles of the Civil War, Hales almost disappears from view, but we know that he was driven from his College, and reduced to pitiful straits. He was forced to dispose even of his books, and the proceeds of the sale, or at least so much as his generosity suffered him to retain, enabled him to return to Eton, and lodge in the house of a widow, whose husband had been his servant. In this retreat he died, on the 19th of May, 1656. According to his express desire, he was buried in the College churchyard, "in plain and simple manner, without any sermon, or ringing the bell, or calling the people together." We have to remember, apart from his claims as a tolerant theologian and large-hearted controversialist, that he was an enthusiastic admirer of Shakespeare's genius. It is recorded of him, that if, in the course of conversation, a topic was introduced as "finely treated by any of the ancient poets," he would undertake to quote something from Shakespeare on the same subject just as well written. Bishop Pearson says of him, that "he was of a nature so kind, so sweet, so courting all mankind—of an affability so prompt, so ready to receive all conditions of men—that I conceive it near as easy a task for any one to become so knowing, or so obliging."

We now pass into the second and smaller quadrangle, the "Green Yard," which is surrounded by a cloister. Here the principal apartments are the spacious and handsome Hall; the Dining-Room for the Fellows on the foundation, with its panelled armorial bearings of provosts and benefactors, its east window representing scenes in the life of Henry VI., and its portraits of distinguished Etonians; and the Library, which contains a very fine collection of books and MSS. Among the former, mention may be made of a richly illustrated copy of Granger's "Biographical History of England;" a vellum Service Book, illuminated, which belonged to Queen Mary, and bears her autograph; a folio copy, on vellum, of the "Nibelungenlied," a gift from the late King of Prussia; and a good copy of the Mazarin Bible. Among the MSS. is a "Heraldic History of the World," with curious illuminated portraits, scenes, and views of places.

Portraits of many famous Etonians (such as Fox, Gray, Canning, Wellington, and Hallam); portraits of most of the Provosts; and of Henry V. and Henry VI., are among the most interesting objects in the Provost's lodgings. If our space permitted, we should gladly stop to discuss with the reader the sayings and doings of the distinguished men who are here represented. We have already referred to Sir Henry Savile, the learned and munificent editor of the works of Chrysostom, and the friend of the Savilian professorships of astronomy and geometry at Oxford; and to Sir Henry Wotton, who, after a stirring career as a diplomatist, spent the later years of his life in this honourable retirement. Wotton, we may add, was both a great German and Italian scholar, and an "amateur and most excellent judge of painting, sculpture, chemistry, and architecture." James I. sent him as ambassador to the Venetian Republic, and he filled similar posts until the very close of the King's reign. He was a stout champion of the cause of Elizabeth, the Queen of Bohemia, who is almost as well known to posterity by Wotton's poetical celebration of her charms as by her own romantic story. Who does not remember the beautiful verses beginning—

> "You meaner beauties of the night,
> That poorly satisfy our eyes
> More by your number than your light!
> You common people of the skies!
> What are you, when the sun shall rise?"

Returning to England in the year before James I.'s death, Wotton was appointed Provost of Eton, and to qualify himself for the post, in strict compliance with the College statutes, he took holy orders, and at the age of fifty-six was ordained deacon. This outward change seems to have brought with it an equally signal inward change. He entered with eagerness on the study of divinity, and gave fervid attention to spiritual exercises. "After his customary public devotions," says Izaak Walton, "his use was to retire into his study, and there to spend some hours in reading the Bible and authors in divinity, closing up his meditations with private prayer; this was, for the most part, his employment in the forenoon. But when he was once sat to dinner, then nothing but cheerful thoughts possessed his mind, and those still increased by constant company at his table of such persons as brought thither additions both of learning and pleasure; but some part of most days was usually spent in philosophical conclusions. Nor did he forget his innate pleasure of angling, which he would usually call 'his idle time not idly spent,' saying often 'he would rather live five May months than forty Decembers.'"

That Wotton was gifted with a keen wit, we know from his famous definition of the duty of an ambassador, "to *lie* abroad for the good of his country."* That his wit was allied to a true sagacity and a wise Catholicity of sentiment, we know from some of his sayings as Provost of Eton. Thus, when asked, "Whether a Papist might be saved?" he answered:—"*You* may be saved without knowing that; look to yourself." Again, overhearing a person who railed loudly against Papists, he exclaimed:—"Pray, sir, forbear till you have studied the points better, for the wise Italians have this proverb, 'He that understands amiss concludes worse.' And take heed of thinking that the further you go from the Church of Rome the nearer you are to God." He had previously given proof, however, that the controversial Romanist was as unwelcome to him as the controversial Protestant. When at home, he attended vespers in one of the churches, and a priest, recognising him, sent him a slip of paper, on which was written:—"Where was your religion to be found before Luther?" He at once wrote the pungent reply:—"My

---

* Walton's saying was in Latin, and the word "mentiendum" does not convey the equivoque which we find in the English "lie."

religion was to be found then, where yours is not to be found now, in the written Word of God."

Wotton died in the autumn of 1639, and it was characteristic of him that he directed the following inscription to be engraved upon his tombstone:—" Hic jacet hujus Sententiæ primus Auctor : '*Disputandi pruritus Ecclesiarum Scabies.*' Nomen alias quære." (Here lies the original author of this sentence : " The itch of controversy is the disease of the Church." His name seek elsewhere.)

To the north of the Tudor structure rise the New Buildings, erected in the same style of architecture, from the designs of Mr. H. Woodyer, in 1847. They contain a Museum, the Boys' Library, and the dormitories for the elder foundation scholars.

The Playing Fields extend to the water's edge; picturesque in themselves, for they are covered with noble trees, and picturesque in their position, which commands delightful views of wood and water, and of Windsor's regal pile. Cricket is a great institution at Eton, but still more famous is it for its aquatic pastimes, which the Thames naturally suggests and provides for. Almost every Etonian can ply his oar with dexterity, and on sunny afternoons the College boats make an agreeable appearance on the river, which, from the Brocas meadow (just above Windsor Bridge) to Surley Hall, three miles up, they apparently regard as their own property. On Speech Day, the 4th of June (the birthday of George III.), and on Election Saturday, the last in July, when the candidates for Cambridge are elected, takes places a grand procession, between the two points just indicated, of all the eight-oar boats; and if the weather be fine, our readers could hardly wish to see a prettier or more interesting spectacle. *Floreat Etona!*

UPTON CHURCH.

We cannot quit Eton without a glance at the "objects of interest" in its neighbourhood. Among these must be reckoned Upton, a pleasant English village, with a fine old church, which of late has been carefully "restored" under the skilful supervision of Mr. Ferrey. It contains some Norman work, especially the west doorway, and the arches between nave and chancel. There are some good brasses in the chancel; and a tablet, attached to one of the tower piers, commemorates Sir William Herschel, the astronomer. Through Upton we make our way to Slough, a long, straggling town, around which a colony of villas and "genteel residences" has, of late years, sprung into existence, and close to which lie the "rose gardens" and nurseries of Messrs. Turner, so well known to amateurs. Off the Windsor road stands Ivy House, now called Herschel's, the residence for forty years of Sir William Herschel. Here he set up his famous forty-foot telescope, and here he made his great surveys of the starry firmament, assisted by his devoted sister, whose labour and love are so agreeably described in the "Memoir of Caroline Herschel." Sir John Herschel was born here, and continued here his astronomical researches until 1840. The illustrious "forty-foot" tube is carefully preserved in the garden.

About three miles to the north of Slough lies Stoke Pogis, the scene of Gray's "Elegy written in a Country Churchyard." Stoke Court, formerly called West Court, "the house in which the poet lived and wrote," was rebuilt in 1845, but no alteration was made in the poet's room. His mother, with a maiden sister, retired here on the death of her husband in 1741. The "Elegy" was begun in the autumn of 1742, but not completed until after the death of his aunt in 1749. It was handed about at first in manuscript, and received, among the higher circles of society, with great applause. When published, it sprang immediately into that favour and popularity which it has ever since retained, and which, in spite of its excessive elaboration and consequent frigidity, it deserves. "I fully agree," says Mr. Leslie Stephen, " with Wolfe [who repeated its beautiful stanzas as his boat dropped down the

STOKE POGIS CHURCH.

St. Lawrence to carry him to the scene of his famous victory and glorious death], that it was a far greater achievement to write the *Elegy* than to storm the heights of Abraham. . . . Gray and his personal admirers seem to have been annoyed at the preference given to this above his other writings. It proved, so he argued, that the stupid public cried for the subject instead of the act; that they liked the *Elegy* as they liked Blair's *Grave*, and would have liked it as well if the same thoughts had been expressed in prose. Undoubtedly the public will always refuse to make that distinction between form and matter which seems so important to the critical mind. It is not, however, that they are unaffected by the artistic skill, but that they are affected unconsciously. The meditations of Blair, of Young, and of Hervey, equally popular in their day, have fallen into disrepute for want of the exquisite felicity of language which has preserved the *Elegy*."

CHURCH PORCH, STOKE POGIS.

Gray was buried in the churchyard to which his genius has given a lasting renown. There,

"Beneath those rugged elms, that yew-tree's shade,
Where heaves the turf in many a mould'ring heap;
Each in his narrow cell for ever laid,
The rude forefathers of the hamlet sleep;"

and the poet sleeps among them, by the side of his mother and his mother's sister. The church is a noble old pile, with a massive "ivy-mantled tower" covered by a wooden spire, and an antique oaken porch. Its chancel is Roman; the nave of various periods of Early English.

The light of Gray's genius also invests with a splendid immortality the Manor House, which, after belonging to the knightly families of the Malins and the Hungerfords, passed into the hands of Henry Hastings, Earl of Huntingdon. By him it was rebuilt in the days of "good Queen Bess." Then it fell to the Crown, and was leased by Sir Edward Coke, who entertained here, in 1601, his aged Sovereign, and died here in 1634. In Gray's time it belonged to Lady Cobham, whose executors sold it to Thomas Penn, son of the great Quaker, and in the Penn family it remained until 1848, when it was purchased by the late Lord Taunton. It is now in the possession of Mr. E. Coleman.

After the publication of the "Elegy," Lady Cobham paid a visit to its author, with the view of making his acquaintance; and as the beginning of this acquaintance had something of a quasi-sentimental character about it, Gray gave a humorous account of it in the verses which he entitled, "A Long Story":—

> "In Britain's isle, no matter where,
> An ancient pile of building stands;
> The Huntingdons and Hattons* there
> Employed the power of fairy hands

> "To raise the ceiling's fretted height,
> Each pannel in achievements clothing,
> Rich windows that exclude the light,
> And passages that lead to nothing."

The "ancient pile," with the exception of one wing, was pulled down in 1789, and the present mansion, in the so-called "classic" style, erected from the designs of the elder Wyatt. It stands in a finely-wooded park, which is enlivened by a shining stream, and diversified by lawn, copse, and leafy knoll. A cenotaph has been erected "in honour of Thomas Gray, amongst the scenes celebrated by that great lyric and elegiac poet," and a column 60 feet high supports a statue of the lawyer-statesman, Sir Edward Coke.

We close our wanderings at Burnham Beeches, which lie about a mile and a-half distant from Stoke Pogis (see Illustration, page 121). "It is a little chaos," says Gray, in reference to this famous spot, the last relic of the vast forest which once overspread the country for miles about, "of mountains and precipices; mountains, it is true, that do not ascend much above the clouds, nor are the declivities quite so amazing as Dover cliff, but just such hills as people who love their necks as well as I do may venture to climb, and crags that give the eye as much pleasure as if they were more dangerous. Both vale and hill are covered with most venerable beeches, and other very reverend vegetables, that, like most other ancient people, are always dreaming out their old stories to the winds—

> "And as they bow their hoary tops, relate,
> In murm'ring sounds, the dark decrees of fate;
> While visions, as poetic eyes avow,
> Cling to each leaf, and swarm on every bough."

The trees are not all beeches, but the majority are, and with their venerable antiquity carry back the spectator in thought to the days when Elizabeth was Queen. Tradition affirms that they were pollarded by Cromwell's soldiers; a process to which is probably due their singularly fantastic growth. Nowhere in the neighbourhood of London shall we find a more romantic or picturesque nook; so infinite are its variations of light and shadow, so complete is its seclusion, so richly tinted is the foliage. Then there are

---

* This is a mistake of the poet's. The Hattons had no connection with Stoke Manor.

hollows brimful of ferns and foxgloves; pools fringed with murmuring rushes; glossy clumps of holly and juniper; winding lanes that seem like Arcadian avenues of greenery, fit only for fairy processions or the haunt of Oreads; and views across a noble common, which just now is bright with golden gorse. No wonder that, a short time since, a general cry of terror arose when it was bruited abroad that "Burnham Beeches" were to be surrendered to the building-mania! Nothing could compensate London for so heavy a loss; and it is pleasant to know that the danger has been, or will be, averted by the public-spiritedness of the Corporation in purchasing the spot, to be preserved in its wild sylvan beauty for all time.

There is a good old Decorated Church at Burnham; the village is quaint and quiet; and to the south lie the remains of the Benedictine Nunnery founded in 1261 by Richard, King of the Romans and Earl of Cornwall.

GRAY'S MONUMENT.—SEE PAGE 142.

Marcus Ward & Co., Royal Ulster Works, Belfast

www.ingramcontent.com/pod-product-compliance
Lightning Source LLC
Chambersburg PA
CBHW031452160426
43195CB00010BB/953